# Praise for
## *On Mended Wings*

*On Mended Wings* captures the heart and soul of this amazing movement of God in Nicaragua. I laughed and I cried at the stories of struggle, hope, and transformation in this book. Never sugarcoating the realities in this often messy process, *On Mended Wings* illustrates how "regular folks" from Nicaragua and North America have experienced the extraordinary with the eyes, hands, and feet of faith.

*-KIM FREIDAH BROWN, PHD, PSYCHOLOGIST, TUCSON, ARIZONA;*
*A MEMBER OF THE NEHEMIAH CENTER TEAM 2002-2010*

It is a risky business to tell the story of transformation in the context of mission. It seems we have an endless capacity to miss the point of how it actually happens. *On Mended Wings* is a trustworthy guide and lifts up a concrete model for us to consider. The Nehemiah Center is a beautiful example of what it means to serve contextually and be led by the Spirit who is at work transforming both people and places in ways that leave us all humbled, hopeful, and grateful.

*-KRIS ROCKE, EXECUTIVE DIRECTOR, CENTER FOR TRANSFORMING MISSION*

The compelling stories in *On Mended Wings* wash over readers like a series of tidal waves, bearing not destruction but transformation, not death but healing. The poor are freed from their bondage to poverty and the rich from their bondage to wealth. This book has the prayer, power, signs and wonders, and energy of Acts 2.

*-JOHN DE HAAN, RETIRED EXECUTIVE DIRECTOR, ASSOCIATION OF EVANGELICAL RELIEF &*
*DEVELOPMENT ORGANIZATIONS (NOW CALLED ACCORD)*

*On Mended Wings* is a hopeful, inspiring, and instructive account of how entire communities can be transformed . . . In beautiful, evocative, and often humorous style, *On Mended Wings* offers penetrating insight into God's transforming work through the extraordinary work of the Nehemiah Center in Nicaragua. May God use this book to inspire many more such centers around the world!

*-SCOTT ALLEN, PRESIDENT, DISCIPLE NATIONS ALLIANCE, INTERNATIONAL SECRETARIAT*

God is doing great things in Nicaragua. The stories of transformation in *On Mended Wings* offer a glimpse of God's new creation. They inspire questions: How might a similar commitment to biblical worldview and collaborative ministry address North American "poverty"? What transformations might God work in the North American world, should we catch this vision? Read it. Be inspired. Dream dreams.

-RYAN FABER, PASTOR OF WORSHIP AND ADMINISTRATION,
FAITH CHRISTIAN REFORMED CHURCH, PELLA, IOWA

Ideas have consequences, and transformation begins with renewing of minds. *On Mended Wings* offers stories of transformation of individuals and communities renewed through the training in biblical world-and-life view of the Nehemiah Center. Read it. Reflect on it. And be prepared for your own transformation.

-REV. LUIS A. PELLECER, LATIN AMERICA REGIONAL DIRECTOR,
CHRISTIAN REFORMED WORLD MISSIONS

*On Mended Wings* offers insightful and often humorous musings as Van Klompenburg journals about her experiences in Nicaragua, discovering the Kingdom of God through the work of the Nehemiah Center and the many Nicaraguan Christians she meets there. Her struggle to make sense of what she experiences helps us to grasp more fully what it means to be transformational workers in that Kingdom and to recognize the mistaken viewpoints we need to cast off along the way.

-JO ANN VAN ENGEN, CO-DIRECTOR, HONDURAS DEVELOPMENT PROGRAM, CALVIN COLLEGE

*On Mended Wings* tells not just the story of the Nehemiah Center, but of the people in Nicaragua, in North America, and around the world whose lives are being transformed as a result of this unique, Spirit-led community of people and organizations. For a world with poverty, injustice, and brokenness, it is a compelling story of a compassionate God, restoring wholeness to individuals, marriages, and families; to churches; to schools; and to barrios, villages and communities.

-BRUCE HEKMAN, PHD, ADJUNCT PROFESSOR OF EDUCATION, CALVIN COLLEGE;
DIRECTOR, INTERNATIONAL CHRISTIAN SCHOOLING INITIATIVE, KUYERS INSTITUTE

A must-read for anyone engaging in cross-cultural missions work—whether long-term or short-term . . . This book helps us see the life-changing experiences that happen as people embark on the ministry of reconciliation in unfamiliar settings where cultural awareness is crucial. *On Mended Wings* covers not only the successes and disappointments of missions work, but also the overall grace of God in the Nicaraguan context.

*-REV. ESTEBAN LUGO, DIRECTOR OF THE OFFICE OF RACE RELATIONS, CHRISTIAN REFORMED CHURCH IN NORTH AMERICA*

With a refreshing blend of both skepticism and hope . . . through vivid and sometimes heart-rending narratives from members of the Nehemiah Center community as well as pointed personal reflections from co-author Carol Van Klompenburg, the book grapples with some of the ongoing critical issues facing development practitioners: How do we avoid dependency? . . . How does lasting change happen? . . . The road toward transformation is long, and the obstacles many, but in these pages the reader also finds reasons for hope.

*-PAMELA NEUMANN, FORMER FOOD FOR THE HUNGRY HUNGER CORPS AND NEHEMIAH CENTER COMMUNICATIONS COORDINATOR 2006-2009*

Through the book, *On Mended Wings,* we see Nicaraguans and North Americans discover how the love of God changes everything: How we understand the world. How we see ourselves. How we act. What we expect . . . Through the eyes of a visitor moving from weary skepticism to refreshed hope, this book tells the stories of those discoveries and their consequences in lives and society. It invites us to consider how we and our communities may also be changed.

*-GIDEON STRAUSS, SENIOR FELLOW, THE CENTER FOR PUBLIC JUSTICE*

# On Mended Wings

*Transforming Lives and Communities in Nicaragua*

By Carol Van Klompenburg with Donna Biddle

ISBN: 978-0-9831961-3-6

Published and printed in the United States of America by The Write Place. Cover and interior design by Alexis Thomas, The Write Place. For more information, please contact:

The Write Place
709 Main Street, Suite 2
Pella, Iowa 50219
www.thewriteplace.biz

Photo credit for butterfly on cover: Dan Vander Beek Photography, Pella, Iowa.

All Scripture quotations are taken from the Holy Bible, New Living Translation, copyright © 1996, 2004, 2007 by Tyndale House Foundation. Used by permission of Tyndale House Publishers, Inc., Carol Stream, Illinois 60188. All rights reserved.

The Nicaragua maps in the Introduction, Chapter 1, and Chapter 10 are used courtesy of the University of Texas Libraries, with adaptations.

Copies of this book may be ordered from The Write Place online at
www.thewriteplace.biz/bookplace

# Contents

# Acknowledgments

It is clearly impossible to acknowledge all the help that I received during the past three years. Every person with whom I have talked about Nicaragua or the Nehemiah Center has in some way helped to make this book possible. I am grateful to all the people I interviewed, who took the time to share their hearts and lives—providing both inspiration and information. I won't name all these people here, but rest assured that all those who shared their lives with me have a permanent place in my heart.

The contributions of some people, however, cry out for more public recognition.

My partners in this process, Joel Huyser and Donna Biddle, have walked alongside me start-to-finish. Joel has been a book shepherd—helping conceptualize its structure and also doing some nitty-gritty work—setting up interviews, providing feedback, interpreting, advising, and fact-checking. Donna Biddle has been a skilled co-writer, a keen-eyed editor who provided an objective viewpoint to balance my passionate one, and a motivator when my energy lagged. Without these two people, *On Mended Wings* would not have been born.

Because my Spanish skills are rudimentary at best, I also relied heavily on a host of translators—many of whom also served as my chauffeurs. My deep thanks goes to Bethany Beachum, Alma Hernández, Josiel Hernández, Judith Hernández, Steve Holtrop, Marcelo Largaespada, Eric Loftsgard, Rolando Mejía, Carl Most, Nathan Sandahl, Jairo Solano, and Melba Vasquez. Their translations and assistance were indispensable.

Thanks also to Luz López, who verified Spanish name spellings, and Marilyn Loftsgard, who assisted Joel with fact-checking and proofreading.

Unless otherwise noted in the captions, the photos on these pages were taken by me during my time in Nicaragua. I'm very grateful to Andje Addink, who graciously consented to the cumbersome task of editing—and sometimes improving—my snapshots.

Thanks to my husband, Marlo, for suggesting during our first Nicaragua visit that in retirement, we regularly volunteer at the Nehemiah Center.

Finally, thanks to my congregational family at Faith Christian Reformed Church, for supporting and expanding on the vision of *On Mended Wings* with its Friends of Chinandega ministry.

# Preface

*In need of mending...*

It's February 2011, and I have just returned from my fourth trip to Nicaragua, the last fact-gathering trip before book publication.

I open my suitcases, still streaked with Nicaragua's ubiquitous dry-season dust, and discover that, despite cushions of newspaper and clothes, one of my ceramic butterflies has cracked in half during the flight.

I'm sad. Out-of-proportion sad.

Five years ago, a butterfly perched on my wrist during morning meditation on my front porch in Iowa, and ever since then I have resonated to butterfly images. A three-foot silk butterfly that emerged from its cocoon week-by-week in our church sanctuary during a sermon series on spiritual disciplines now hangs in my sun porch.

On this latest Nicaragua trip, I had admired the ceramic butterflies perched on cement toadstools in the courtyard of Managua's Nehemiah Center and asked where I could purchase them. Juan Granados, the Nehemiah Center's business manager, told me that crafts people made them at Masaya, an hour or so to the southeast. "Great!" I said. "Our team is traveling there next Friday."

The following Monday, however, a proudly smiling Juan presented me with three ceramic butterflies. He reassured me that he did not make a special trip. He was passing through Masaya on the weekend to visit relatives and stopped for this purchase.

I was touched. I had only a nodding acquaintance with Juan. I was quite certain that, as a percentage of income, those butterflies cost him more than they would have cost me. I asked if I could reimburse him for the cost. No, he insisted, they were a gift. It was his pleasure. Truly.

The moment etched itself in gold letters on my heart. I thanked him profusely. I wrote him a thank-you card.

Juan, I learned later, had—just prior to my arrival—purchased and placed those butterfly-and-toadstool ornaments in the courtyard, with varied reactions from the staff members. The Nicaraguan staff had thought they were a wonderful focal point. The North Americans had been a little less enthusiastic.

My admiration had validated Juan's taste.

I learned about this varied reaction when our service-and-learning team decided to investigate distributing these yard ornaments in the United States as a fundraiser.

And now, this butterfly—hand-painted in vibrant Latino colors, an unexpected gift, an emblem of different cultural tastes, a harbinger of future hopes—has lost its wing.

Marlo, my solution-oriented, engineer husband, picks up the pieces, nests them together, turns them over, and pronounces the wing repairable. "I can glue it and reinforce the bottom with a metal strip," he says. "From above, it will hardly show."

My broken butterfly can be mended and made new.

If only a little glue and a strip of metal could repair Nicaragua.

Or, for that matter, North America.

That task belongs to Bigger Hands.

And in those hands—to paraphrase Gandhi's maxim—perhaps I can be just one glue-drop of the transformation I hope to see.

# Introduction
## In Search of a Bigger World

*Nicaragua: a small country that provided a bigger world*

In January 2008, weary of managing the small business I had started, and bored with the jaded formulas of my Kuyperian-Calvinist, every-square-inch-belongs-to-God theology, I was ready for a change. Along with my husband, Marlo, I opted to join a service-and-learning team from my Pella, Iowa, congregation traveling to the Nehemiah Center in Nicaragua's capital city, Managua.

Pre-trip, asked to share my overriding fear with the team, I said, "Getting sick." Our first day there, asked to share my hopes, I said, "A bigger world."

In the next ten days, both came true.

Attacked by Montezuma's revenge, I gazed listlessly out the van windows en route from Managua to Santa Lucia and wondered why on God's green earth I was sweating in the dust of this God-forsaken country. Arriving at our primitive quarters, from my lumpy bed I heard, unmoved, a distant drama in the adjacent room over a saucer-sized spider. My universe had shrunk to my internal processes.

Before and after that nadir, however, I was stretched beyond belief by a land as foreign to a middle-class Midwesterner as another universe.

Accustomed to the silence and open space of Iowa prairies, already between the Managua airport and the Nehemiah Center, my senses were assaulted by a crowded cacophony. Busses, trucks, motorcycles, and taxis roared and honked along narrow streets, often within inches of pedestrians. Diesel exhaust fumes invaded the open windows. At stoplights, street vendors hawked bottled water, sugared drinks, watches, tourist trinkets, and snacks. Others washed windshields hoping for a tip, sometimes even after the driver had said no. Some simply begged.

Downtown Managua has only two buildings left usable after the 1972 earthquake. The rest have not been rebuilt. Squatters inhabit some of the downtown shells still standing. Others live wall-to-wall in black plastic shanties. I was assaulted by street-after-bumpy-street of grinding poverty peppered with corner *pulperias* (in-home shops) and street-side tortilla stands where

*Carol at work in the Nehemiah Center courtyard kiosko*

vendors eke out an existence.

Outside of downtown, the residential areas are a nonstop series of walls, gates, and fences with a guard dog behind each. In the better homes, an armed guard keeps watch day and night.

Just such a guard opened the huge, iron gate to the Nehemiah Center campus as we headed for our dormitory-style bunks for our first night.

I woke at dawn to the alarm of roosters, cattle, dogs, and traffic. With only cold water available and unwilling to water-torture my entire body, I bent my waist at right-angles for an icy shampoo and followed up with a sponge bath. I walked on a ceramic tile floor, which I later learned is mopped daily, to fetch clothes from a dank, rough-surfaced wood closet. I brushed my teeth with bottled water. I learned to deposit toilet paper in the adjacent wastebasket, rather than flushing it. At night the faint bathroom smell drifted toward my upper bunk.

Under a grass-roofed *ranchón*, I breakfasted in open air each morning on beans and rice, and oh-so-sweet, tree-ripened fruit—mangoes, bananas, and white pineapple.

Part of our ten days we worked: We planted one hundred fifty bougainvilleas along the Nehemiah Center's back perimeter, an attractive disguise for the barbed wire fence. We sewed curtains and painted walls at Tesoros de Dios, a school for children with special needs. At Santa Lucia, a rural mountain village two hours east of Managua in Nicaragua's volcanic mountain range, we helped pour a cement floor for a church, under the leadership of local experts.

We also toured. We ferried among the 365 tiny islands of Lake Nicaragua, Central America's largest lake. Laguna de Apoyo and the Mombacho rain forests wowed us with grand vistas and tropical beauty. I met my favorite houseplants in their natural habitat.

Along with the rest of the team, I also attended training sessions and learned about the nation's poverty, illiteracy, and religious perspectives. It is into this context, we learned, that the Nehemiah Center—a practicing community of collaborative faith and a biblical worldview—brings its transforming vision.

When I heard the term "biblical worldview," I was back in familiar territory—finally. And I alternated between the ho-hum and the smirk that had become a more typical response in recent decades than I had admitted, even to myself.

On my college campus back in the rebellious and turbulent 1960s, my personal rebellion took the form of a triumphal Kuyperian Calvinism: With the supreme narcissistic confidence of youth, I knew my fellow graduates and I would conquer every square inch for Christ. Soon. Very soon.

As decade followed decade, I continued to hear—and use—the same rhetoric. In those decades, I saw little change, at least not in my square inch.

And now this rhetoric had reappeared—in Nicaragua.

Oh, well . . . The rhetoric was only a fly in the ointment. On this, my first experience in Nicaragua, I was already seeing new horizons, new challenges.

In the debriefing session before we left Nicaragua to return to the United States, Steve Holtrop, Nehemiah Center's coordinator for service-and-learning teams, suggested we think through short and long versions of our trip story, and then choose the appropriate one, depending on our listener's level of interest. "Not everyone will be interested in an hour-long recital," he warned us. "Remember, life back home has been going along as normal." He also suggested that we consider how this trip might affect our lives back home. The trip purpose was two-way transformation. This had been, after all, a service-*and-learning* team.

Short or long, I did not know which tale to tell: Exotic tropical beauty? Wilderness adventure? Dire poverty? Personal illness? The Nehemiah Center's mission and vision?

It was a tangled tale.

A few days earlier, my husband, Marlo, had said to me, "When I retire next year, I can see volunteering here a month each January." I had readily agreed.  I'd be able to escape a month of Iowa winter and be somehow useful as well.

With all its challenges, I was drawn to this strange, new world that enlarged mine.

Yes, it was a tangled tale, but this much I knew: I wanted to return.

## Naively Suggesting a Niche

The first day back in Iowa, I pulled a sieve from my kitchen cupboard and was overwhelmed with a wave of deep and absurd gratitude for that piece of plastic. I felt like Eustace in C.S. Lewis' *The Voyage of the Dawn Treader,* stripped of dragon-scales to naked flesh.

I wrote in my journal that my best words for the team trip were "touched" and "a momentous underground tectonic shift I do not yet understand."

In that cloud of unknowing, I began to dream dreams of writing a book.

My most satisfying project in recent years had been the co-authoring with Donna Biddle a biography of Gary and Matilda Vermeer, *In Search of a Better Way,* commissioned by Vermeer Corporation as this amazing Christian couple approached their ninetieth birthdays.

Why not another book project—a book about the Nehemiah Center?

In a naïve burst of enthusiasm, I imagined a process and emailed a book proposal to team coordinator Steve Holtrop and Nehemiah Center cofounder Joel Huyser.  I asked Donna Biddle to again co-author with me, and she said yes.  One month and many email exchanges later, we signed a three-way agreement.

I would gather information during another church team visit in June 2009 and again during our first month-long volunteer trip in January 2010.

With Donna as a writing partner, I had found my Nicaragua niche.

## Meeting Maria

On my first interviewing foray, in June 2009, I met the coffee farmers of Mount Mombachito.

Partners Worldwide coordinators David and Wendy Van Klinken drove me nearly three hours northeast from Managua over increasingly rough roads, until finally we hairpinned up the side of the extinct volcano. On the way, I learned about the six farmers who grew coffee on loaned land that they would eventually buy. We parked the truck, sprayed every square inch of our skin with insect repellent, grabbed water bottles, and walked the crater's treacherous paths from farm to farm, heeding the farmers' warnings to watch out for slippery banana leaves.

The houses blurred together in a steady stream until we reached the home of Maria Luisa.

A stone walk led us to the front door of the three-room house where she and Lucas lived with nine of their thirteen children.  Mouth slightly sunken above a strong chin, skin weathered, Maria looked all of her forty-eight years. But she sat erect on the hand-hewn bench along the wall of her home, with the dignity befitting a community matriarch. Lucas, a shy man who had kindly offered to shoulder my computer case, sat silent at her side.

As a guest, I was shown to a plastic chair in the center of the room. At first her home looked just like all the others. Then I noticed a difference. The wall behind Maria was covered with newspaper.

Thinking of the inch-wide cracks between the boards in other homes, I asked, "Are the newspapers to keep out the wind?"

"No, they are for decoration," she said.

For decoration. Newspapers.

Inside of me, time stopped.

But Maria talked on, telling me of the milk candies she made and sold. She showed me the colorful saddlebags her daughter was weaving to sell.

At first her words came from a distance, muffled by the drumbeat in my head: Newspapers. For decoration.

When I was able to look up from the saddlebags, I saw that her eyes were bright with pleasure and pride.

In this moment, God transformed my eyes and ears, and in Maria, I saw myself.

Maria had an artist's soul. What I did with houseplants, Maria did with newspapers. What I did with perennials, she did with stones rescued from a government road dig.

Later that day, the Van Klinkens told me a North American once asked Maria what she would do if someone gave her a million dollars. "I think I would die," she had said, grinning. "But if I survived, I'd buy a picture for my wall."

## Finding a Voice

In the remainder of that June trip, and during our subsequent month-long stay in January 2010, I asked questions and keystroked the answers. But those words, thousands upon thousands of them, were words of others, not my own.

Though I did not understand—and could not express—what these experiences meant to me, I knew I was seeing glimpses of glory. The most beautiful room in architect Gloria Saballos' tiny house was reserved for prayer alone. Pastor Tomás Ruiz, when he saw that God loved servant-hearted obedience more than worshipping and fasting, gathered his entire neighborhood together and publicly apologized. Daniel Aragón and his wife freely gave away a plot of land they had purchased to build a home.

For a few days that month, Marlo and I joined team members from Faith Christian Reformed Church of Burlington, Ontario, Canada, as they explored a possible five-year relationship with companion churches in León. At a Poneloya beach hotel, exhausted after a long day, we left our cramped and stifling rooms for group conversation in a circle of chairs overlooking the ocean. I don't remember the conversation clearly, and I was too tired to journal about it later, but the Canadians talked in hushed voices about all that we had seen and heard that day. They talked of how a Canadian-Nicaraguan church relationship might look.

Somewhere, amid the heat and sweat and exhaustion, after months of muteness, I found words. I stumbled through a few quavering sentences. To the best of my memory, they were something like this: "In people here, I see something I do not understand. When Nicaraguans see God as God of all, something HAPPENS. Their lives are changed. They act. It makes a difference. They have much, much to teach me. I have learned much, and I am only just beginning."

I fell back to wordless silence, and the conversation continued in the distance. I thought more about what I had seen and heard: changed lives, risk taking, sharing, a freedom to give, friendship, community . . . Finally, I knew—or perhaps simply knew again—that seeing the world as belonging to God offered a wonderful window for my heart, in which he chose to make his home. I knew, too, that no home's window to the world is totally clear. Nicaraguans' worldviews had been dirt-smeared by the idols of their culture, but so had mine. It still was!

After the conversation dwindled, I returned to my room. The window had a broken pane. The ceiling fan failed to turn. The toilet did not flush. A pancake-sized welt on my forearm itched.

I bedded down with a Canadian woman I met just yesterday, threw off the stifling top sheet, lay still, and tried not to scratch. I fought for sleep.

I recalled Nigerian missionary Robert Recker's speech to my Iowa Sunday School class when I was eleven. He showed jungle slides and issued a challenge: "Maybe God is calling you to the mission field!"

I had been terrified. Please, God, don't call me to be a missionary to primitive and bug-infested Africa. Please. Please! PLEASE!

He didn't. He graciously called me to writing instead.

Now, fifty years later, he sent me to Central America, definitely bug-infested and, in some areas, still primitive—at least to my North American eyes. I knew, despite the bugs and heat and exhaustion, I would return, not because Nicaragua needed me, but because I needed Nicaragua.

I had expected Nicaragua to give me a bigger world, and it did. I had not expected it to change my heart.

I knew that, at long last, I had begun to find my words.

Somewhere in the darkness, I thought I heard a chuckle.

*Carol Van Klompenburg*
March 2011

# On Mended Wings

*Transforming Lives and Communities in Nicaragua*

By Carol Van Klompenburg with Donna Biddle

Pastor Tomás Ruiz

# 01

## Just Another Conference

*I still see the burdens. They touch a pastor's heart. You can't fix them instantly or at one time.*

- *PASTOR TOMÁS RUIZ*

Wedged inside a sweltering bus heading into Managua—Nicaragua's capital city of more than a million people—Pastor Tomás Ruiz felt his thoughts rushing in his head, as noisy and chaotic as the traffic around him. At each stop, more and more people squeezed onto the already overcrowded bus, and yet, as oppressive as it was crammed into this bus, his thoughts seemed worse.

Just thirty-six years old in 1999, Tomás was feeling defeated, burdened.

For fourteen years, he had pastored *Faro de Luz Iglesia* (Lighthouse Church) in Los Brasiles—a *comarca* (semi-rural area) twenty kilometers northwest of the nation's capital. For all those fourteen long years, he had preached at daily services, prayed far into the night, and fasted for weeks. He had preached energetically about the evils and worldliness of the surrounding community.

Despite his efforts, however, his church had never grown beyond twenty-five members. And none of those members could be bothered to serve the church. Tomás himself did all the preaching, singing, praying, and even cleaning. In his prayers, Tomás often told God of his longing for growth, needing thirty members to qualify as a full-fledged congregation in his *Evangelio Completo* (Full Gospel) denomination. In his desperation, he sometimes talked to people on the streets and then listed them on church rolls, even though they never showed up.

Here he was on this day heading toward yet another pastors' conference in a city that seemed to overflow with pastors' conferences. For certain, Tomás had attended his share in the past. He had even attended one about Greek and Hebrew words—"Too lofty for a simple man like me,"

Tomás remembered.

Only his sense of politeness had compelled him to attend today's conference. He hadn't wanted to offend the North American friend who had invited him. But that politeness couldn't keep him from privately thinking, "Here we go again. Just another conference."

Tomás, small and slender by North American standards, is a humble man with handsome features. He grew up in a small, rural community in the province of León, and lives in a small house with concrete floors and meager furnishings with his wife, three children, and one grandson.

In his community of Los Brasiles, many of the inhabitants are employed in garment assembly factories, where typical wages are $125 per month, an income that Nicaraguans can stretch creatively to meet basic needs. Although local wage scales are low, the employment rate in Los Brasiles, by Nicaraguan standards, is high.

Within Los Brasiles, Tomás lives in the San Francisco *barrio* (neighborhood), one of eight barrios in the community of several thousand people. In Tomás's barrio, 850 people live in just 146 houses. Seventy of these are two-generation families living together.

Like many Nicaraguan pastors, Tomás does not have an advanced theological education.

*Tomás Ruiz in secondary school media classroom*

Before becoming a pastor, he worked in a machete *fabrica* (factory), spending the last fifteen minutes of his half-hour lunchtime at the factory preaching to fellow employees. He did that until 1985, when he felt called to become a full-time pastor.

As a pastor, during fasting and prayer, he sensed God's hand leading him, but he couldn't quite grasp it. He heard God tell him to disciple the congregation. Although he scolded the congregation, he was still doing all the church work alone. He heard God telling him that the physical life was important, along with the spiritual life. Once, he recalled, he preached that prosperity was important, that it was God's will for his people. It was an exciting message, and his congregation responded with enthusiasm, raising their voices and clapping their hands. When he got home, there was nothing to eat.

It wasn't that Tomás had given up. In fact, he had started ministries. With help from the

North American-based Missionary Ventures, he had founded feeding centers and children's Bible clubs. With help from Habitat for Humanity, he administered a grant that brought new houses to the community. He tried not to become disheartened when his congregation objected because some of those houses were provided to people outside of the congregation.

Submitted photo

*Los Brasiles residents clean their village.*

"I had heard it said that a person who has vision will achieve success, and that a church without vision has no future, but I did not understand what that meant," he remembered.

With all these things on his mind, Tomás headed into Managua to attend the conference in June of 1999.

## Affected to the Core

In their culture, Nicaraguans are prone to more dramatic life changes than most North Americans feel comfortable with. Skeptical Americans often are suspicious, doubtful. In Tomás's case, this conference led him to a dramatic conversion that was both immediate and ongoing.

At last, he not only saw God's hand leading him into new directions, but he could finally grasp it firmly.

"I arrived, started participating, and I was affected to my *corazon* (core or heart)," he said. "I never missed a day. I was stoked to learn this stuff because they taught about working and serving in the community. I came back *embarazado* (pregnant or overflowing) with many ideas."

Following the conference, Tomás spent a year studying with the same friend who had invited him—Eric Loftsgard of Missionary Ventures. With other pastors, they studied *Discipling Nations: The Power of Truth to Transform Cultures,* a book by Darrow Miller that many have said led to new thinking.

Tomás also received subsequent Community Health Evangelism (CHE) training, which helped him better understand the impact a church could make in its community. For once, his motivation wasn't forced. "I kept going, not because I was obligated, but because I was excited."

Like others who attended that 1999 conference, Tomás began learning about "biblical worldview," a term he had never heard, or at least had never taken note of, before that conference. He was coming to understand that the world belonged to God. Every day. Everywhere. Not just in the church. Not just during services. For Tomás, it was a change of life: he was made new.

## Reaching His Community

For six months, Tomás spent as much time as he could in intense prayer and fasting. Then he organized an outdoor community meeting in his San Francisco barrio, a social gathering complete with food and conversation. Standing before the people gathered around him—his family, friends, and neighbors, many of whom he had known for years—Tomás apologized.

"I asked forgiveness for not living up to my responsibility to be a light to the community," Tomás said. "I apologized for how I treated the community, how I judged them and condemned them." He told them he lacked the heart of a servant that Jesus had said he must have.

In a very public way that day, Tomás asked for forgiveness. He promised to change his attitude and his service.

And one of the first changes he made? He cut the frequency of his church services. Instead of asking members to attend daily services, he cut back to just three per week, hoping to allow them more time to spend with their families and community.

At first the community did not respond, church member Liset Martinez recalled. Suspicions ran deep.

"The first thing we noticed was that our pastor's leadership style changed," Liset said. "Before this he demanded and screamed at people to get them to do things in the church."[1] Tomás started to talk about a vision of service. The congregation started to catch the vision. And Tomás started visiting homes of community residents.

Three church members agreed to head *Grupos de Rescate* (rescue teams) to meet with other people in the community and talk to them about the church's new vision. "They were very scared," said Tomás. "They were meeting with the community people we had been condemning."

Each leader founded a ten-member group that met regularly for conversation and food. Out of the group meetings came the vision for community cleanup. In their thirty-four-year existence, Los Brasiles' streets had never been cleaned of garbage, either by residents or county agencies.

"Early one Sunday morning we started cleaning, putting our hands into rotten stinking puddles with worms in them. People asked why, and we told them that this is the way the church

---

[1] "Church Action in Transforming a Community, Faro de Luz: in Los Brasiles: A case study from Nicaragua," Christian Reformed World Relief Committee, February 2004.

responds to community health needs," Tomás said.

With Community Health Evangelism (CHE) training, church members had learned that the community's frequent cases of child diarrhea were transmitted through contact with garbage on the streets and yards. To reduce disease, they removed the cause. When the region's government saw the initiative, it sent trucks to transport the collected garbage to the dumps. Tomás said matter-of-factly, "Since 2002, Los Brasiles has not had any cases of diarrhea caused by garbage in the community."

When members of the congregation learned that dengue—a painful disease that could occasionally lead to fatal complications—was caused by mosquitoes breeding in stagnant puddles, they filled those puddles, reducing dengue frequency. The government responded by constructing curbs to improve water drainage.

Team leaders also began passing on the healthy home training they had received from CHE, basic things like sanitation, nutrition, establishing kitchen gardens, and water purification. Homes practicing appropriate levels of good hygiene received certificates.

Tomás's church, Faro de Luz, had envisioned sixty people in rescue teams within a year. It overshot that target by thirty. People began to realize that money wasn't always required to make a difference.

## Growing in Ministry

Meanwhile, Tomás continued a small feeding center and a Bible club. As the months went by, momentum continued to build for better conditions. Hungry for better education for their children, residents asked more frequently about a preschool. Fearing rejection, Tomás asked the Department of Education for permission to launch a preschool. To his surprise, officials gladly consented, saying they had difficulty providing enough preschools.

So, the pastor who had condemned education as worldly began hosting preschool classes under a thatched roof attached to the back of his home. Its retention rate was double that of government preschools, and it won government recognition. One preschool became three.

As the Bible clubs grew to five hundred members, taught by volunteer teachers, the church started considering a primary school. At first, Tomás wondered about the wisdom of this idea. "We asked the neighbor about buying his land, but it was expensive. Then I got another word from the Lord: 'You have difficulty because my people are not tithing. They are just flicking out a coin here and there.' I shared this word with the congregation, and in one Sunday they donated a third of the required money. Then I knew that we could move ahead."

Faro de Luz began holding primary school classes outdoors before construction started. To decide on a tuition rate, church members surveyed the community door-to-door to determine what was affordable and appropriate. Several years later, Compassion International, a Christian advo-

*External hallway of Faro de Luz Christian School in Los Brasiles*

cacy ministry, partnered with the church to start an after-school program in the Faro de Luz facilities. However, Compassion restricted its program to two hundred fifty children, half of those who wished to enroll. The solution? The church enrolled two hundred fifty children in the program, and leaders then volunteered their time to tutor the other two hundred fifty children in a different time slot.

The Nehemiah Center, also launched from that 1999 conference in Managua, came alongside the church, sending a team to assist in the first phase of construction. "That was a beautiful experience," remembered Tomás. "The North American team helped with funding, and worked alongside church members. And community people worked too—without pay! We just fed them. It was amazing to see how the Lord brought them all together. I thank God that a poor community is rich in the Lord."

And, throughout this time, the programs continued expanding. In earlier days, Tomás had condemned sports, believing sports to be worldly and therefore in opposition to the church. Now, however, he embraced sports as an opportunity to reach out. The church created an outdoor sports court and sponsored tournaments.

Today, school enrollment tops 170. A vocational school, built on a corner of the grounds, provides training in metalworking. More than a dozen computers line the walls of one classroom for technical training. Gang membership and crime have declined. "We have things around here that could be stolen, but they aren't," said Tomás. The government has continued to respond to community initiatives, putting in streetlights and more reliable water pumps.

Sitting at a desk in the school he helped launch, Tomás remembered how he used to dream of expensive evangelical campaigns to increase his church membership. Instead, he went to work in his Father's world—and his church has swelled to more than eight times its previous size. It has also launched two daughter churches.

The path hasn't always been smooth. There have been struggles, even confrontations with his denomination over differing visions and his perceived "worldliness." Then, two years ago, the leader of the Evangelio Completo denomination came to him, asked for forgiveness, and the breach was healed.

"People have started coming and asking how we could do this, what was happening here. This gave me an opportunity to teach biblical worldview to eighty different churches and their leaders. We attracted the same kind of pastors I used to be," Tomás said.

Today, instead of relying on the overcrowded and often unreliable bus transportation, Tomás travels and speaks from time to time using a motorcycle provided for him by the Christian Motorcycle Association, a provision the organization has made for more than fifty Nicaraguan pastors.

## Ongoing Burdens

The story that Tomás tells is a powerful one. Yet, as he sat in that school desk, Tomás spoke matter-of-factly, humbly, without any swelling self-importance. A serious and reserved man, he rarely jokes, yet his smile is broad and frequent. He wouldn't hesitate to give the white, Nicaraguan dress shirt off his back. He talked of his continuing passion and vision.

"I have the burden of always wanting to serve, to keep the church moving and involved. It drives me to constant prayer."

Prayer fueled the vision that finally enabled his church to live up to its denominational name—Evangelio Completo, the Full Gospel. Over the past decade, Tomás has come to understand that the walls he built to protect his church from his community were actually prison walls that constrained his church from growing outward. Struggles will continue, but with God's help, Tomás and many others like him who have made the important connection between God and his world will continue to transform their lives, their churches, and their communities in ways that only God knows.

Walking alongside them in that transformation is *Centro Nehemías*—the Nehemiah Center.

*Even the architecture of the Nehemiah Center encourages collaboration.*

# 02

## A Community for Transformation

*Be the change you wish to see in the world.*

*- MAHATMA GANDHI*

The man whom Pastor Tomás Ruiz didn't want to offend by missing the biblical worldview conference was Eric Loftsgard. A lean, strong man, Eric can be intimidating. He waves his arms extensively when he talks, and he speaks with authority, forcefully. He's a technical, mechanical man, a type-A personality, who gets things done on time and on budget.

Twenty years ago, back in his home state of Oregon, Eric was a successful home builder—a contractor who built gorgeous homes, working in a boom time in a boomtown. He and his wife, Marilyn, lived the good life as North Americans know it—a life of luxury with trucks, boats, motor homes, and motorcycles.

They were self-described, back-pew-on-Sunday-morning Christians.

They believe their transformation started shortly after their second daughter, Jackie, was born. The catalyst was two men who worked for Eric at the time. "One was hyper, a Holy-Ghost charismatic," Eric recalled. "The other was an ultra, fire-breathing, Bible-thumping, conservative, independent Baptist. They were the two extremes of denominational poles and both worked for me. There were sparks flying every day, and I was in the middle. I was the moderator and the referee. Boy, I learned so much, and it was what made me question my faith."

One of those men was a pastor. His wife brought Marilyn a meal after Jackie's birth. "No one had ever done that," Marilyn recalled. "I was floored. For me, it was out of gratitude that I said, 'Let's go visit his church.' He preached on the Lamb of God, and scales went away from our eyes and from that point on, life was never the same."

Marilyn couldn't get enough of God's word, hungry for it and eagerly looking forward to church services on Sunday mornings, Sunday nights, and Wednesday nights. Eric became so

*Marilyn and Eric Loftsgard*

enthused that in 1995, he started going on mission trips.

At about the same time, the houses that Eric built stopped selling, money became tight, and the couple started questioning the direction of their lives. At one point, a friend told Marilyn that she thought God was calling the couple to be missionaries. "That thought had never entered my mind. I remember where I was standing. I about dropped the phone.

"We were trying to figure out what we would do. Eric said then, 'What if we give it all to God? What if he sends us to Africa and we have to live in Africa?'

"And I said, 'He will never do that. Why would he send us?'"

By March 1997, the couple was ready to be sent, not to Africa but to Central America. Shortly before Eric's mission trip that month to Nicaragua, they told their church they believed that God was calling them to be missionaries.

"I picked him up from the airport, and I asked how was it? He said that is where we were supposed to go. I remember thinking I should be freaking out, but I had peace."

When the couple heard God's call to Nicaragua in 1997 as missionaries, Marilyn and Eric Loftsgard thought they had been transformed.

When they arrived in Nicaragua in August 1998, they found their transformation was only beginning.

# Nehemiah Center– A Place of Collaboration

Located on an 8.7-acre wooded campus it shares with a Christian school and a vocational training center, the Nehemiah Center building is a 10,000-square-foot quadrangle of offices and meeting rooms surrounding an open courtyard with a tile-roofed gazebo in the center. It was completed in 2007 with labor mostly by local Nicaraguans and built with funds provided by Missionary Ventures through a donation by a

*The kiosko in Nehemiah Center courtyard is the site of many meetings.*

couple from Milwaukee, Wisconsin. Partners Worldwide provided funding for the land for both the Nehemiah Center and the adjacent Nicaragua Christian Academy-Nejapa, an affordable Spanish-speaking Christian school.

This is the Nicaraguan office base of a half-dozen international Christian agencies that have agreed to share space and a whole lot more.

Adjacent to the office quadrangle are a guest house and a *ranchón* (large open space with a thatched roof) where short- and medium-term visitors live and eat. Some visitors are college students taking courses or doing internships. Others are service-and-learning teams who come to partner with the international and national agencies.

---

## AT A GLANCE
### *Nehemiah Center Mission and Values*

Identity:
 The Nehemiah Center is a multicultural community of learning, service, and collaboration, comprised of three teams: an international team, an administrative support team, and a training and consulting team composed of Nicaraguan leaders (the Ezra team).

Vision:
 We see individuals, churches, organizations, and local communities who are putting into practice the values of a biblical worldview and who are learning, serving, and collaborating together for the transformation of both their own lives and the broader society.

Mission:
 To develop integral agents of transformation who are grounded in a Christ-centered, biblical worldview and woven into local, vocational, and global networks of learning, service, and collaboration for the transformational development of communities and nations.

Values:
 · Biblical worldview
 · Holistic transformational development
 · Equipping agents of transformation
 · Collaboration
 · Teamwork
 · Servant leadership
 · Persistent prayer
 · Training and development of local leaders
 · Transparency and stewardship in the use and management of finances
 · Renewal of the family, school, business, government, and local church

Submitted photo

*Kim Freidah Brown pauses in front of a poster that includes a silhouette of General Sandino.*

All the agencies and staff are committed to the Nehemiah Center mission statement: "To develop integral agents of transformation who are grounded in a Christ-centered, biblical worldview and woven into local, vocational, and global networks of learning, service, and collaboration for the transformational development of communities and nations."

As she sat in the *kiosko* (gazebo) in the Nehemiah Center courtyard, Kim Freidah Brown gazed at the quadrangle of surrounding offices and the open-air, wrap-around hallway with its red-tiled floor. Kim, who served fifteen years in Nicaragua, most recently as country director for Food for the Hungry (FH), took a stab at defining the center. "We are not a center or a building. We are . . . " She paused, seeking words for the complexity. "We are a community, a vibrant community. We share the vision of seeking this outrageous goal—the transformation of Nicaragua. Outsiders might say it is absurd, but we are seeking the restoration and transformation of all things."

Kim leaned back in the wooden rocking chair and looked around again at the building: "Despite our name, we now see ourselves more as a community than a center. Center means a building, and community is about those relationships. We now have a beautiful center, but what defines us is this community."

Kim isn't alone in her struggle to define what the Nehemiah Center has become.

"You can't identify what this is," said Eric. "It is not a Bible school, not a training center. Ultimately we call ourselves a community, and people have a hard time with that, a community of learning, service, and collaboration . . . There is not a phrase that sums this community all up. We are the body of Christ here with all the unique members, and everyone all contributes something unique and specific that not one organization could have."

Daniel Boniche, a native Nicaraguan and the center's current director, described it similarly: "A center of service, learning, and collaboration, where everybody interacts with everybody

## The Nehemiah Center as Starfish

Missionary Ventures representative Eric Loftsgard often consults books to help him understand situations around him. So, it was not surprising when Eric borrowed a concept from a book to explain the organization of the Nehemiah Center. This illustration is from *The Starfish and the Spider: The Unstoppable Power of Leaderless Organizations*, by Ori Brafman and Rod A. Beckstrom. As Eric explains it, if you cut off the head of a spider organization, it dies. Spider organizations are hierarchical, and quite often a heavy hand at each level controls the level below it.

Starfish organizations, on the other hand, are decentralized. Cut off an arm, and it continues to live. Some starfish species may even form another starfish. A starfish, Eric says, is what the Nehemiah Center has become.

*Francisco Gutiérrez*     *Daniel Boniche*

else. [We are a group of] different entities, but we all have a similar mission and vision, and we each make our own contribution to this vision and mission. We do this without losing the individual character of each of the entities but by collaborating with each other."

"What is the difference between the Nehemiah Center and others? It is a space of learning," said Francisco Gutiérrez, a founder and current board president of the Nehemiah Center as well as former director of *Accion Medica Cristiana* (Christian Medical Action), a Nicaraguan Christian development agency that often works with the Nehemiah Center on joint projects. "No one says they have the total truth. So, we can tell others what we have learned or have read. It is a space where you can give and receive at the same time."

The center came about because native Nicaraguans as well as missionaries and representatives from different organizations, from different denominations, and with different philosophies were willing to come together to discover their sameness and develop a vision of transformation.

Through this proocess, they discovered their similarities and set aside their differences.

But that is not as simple as it sounds. Getting people and organizations with passionate interests to collaborate is never simple. It is like the prophet Nehemiah's task to rebuild the city of Jerusalem—impossible—except for the fact that nothing is impossible with God.

"Sometimes we need to put aside our human nature, break down our walls, and become open to what God wants from us.

## Choosing a Name, Discovering a Purpose

The Nehemiah Center name was chosen fairly quickly, according to Ken Ekstrom, one of the founders. "We needed a name that was not already in use. One other group was using the Nehemiah Center name. Joel [Huyser] talked with them and we decided it would not be an issue."

To distinguish the new center from the other organization, a longer name was created: The Nehemiah Center for Transformational Development. "Nehemiah was a nation builder, rebuilding what had been Jerusalem, rebuilding the country, rebuilding lives," said Ken.

The center was incorporated in April 2002, but the people involved began talking about themselves as the Nehemiah Center as early as 2000, according to Joel Huyser, another one of the founders. Rebuilding was an important concept to them.

"Because of my [theological] background, I began to talk about a philosophy of societal development that sees as key the building of strong and healthy institutions in different sectors of society," said Joel. He believed that sustainable community development required not just healthy churches, but healthy families, healthy schools, and healthy businesses. "So, we then began to think how we could expand from working with churches and families into other areas of society."

It's a continual effort against thinking of the work as *my* ministry, *my* mission, *my* focus," said Wendy Van Klinken, who along with her husband, David, served with Partners Worldwide in Nicaragua.

Added Pastor John Lee, a Christian Reformed Church missionary who served in Nicaragua from 2001 through 2004: "The unity among missionary communities here is unusual . . . In some fields, missionaries can be territorial, but here there is a real mutual respect and they tell each other, 'I know someone who can help you.' The Nehemiah Center wouldn't work in a place where the attitude is 'I'm doing my thing. Go away.' "

"No one owns or controls this," said Eric. "We can't say the Christian Reformed Church controls this or runs that, or Missionary Ventures doesn't control this or run that. The beauty of an equal collaboration is where everyone's voice counts and we arrive at consensus.

"[The central beliefs] are what bind us together, and if you truly believe these, you can become a partner," said Eric. "The money always seems to just fill in. There is no set demand: thou shalt pay X. As you share the vision, as people buy in, the money has always come in various amounts and at various times from various organizations. We have always met that year's budget as God saw fit. It is stressful preparing budgets on faith income, but it works. It works."

Key to this success, however, are the beliefs, the relationships. "It has to start with individuals building a relationship. Even though we have institutionalized this, the institution came after the relationships, and the relationships remain the core," said Kim Freidah Brown.

That's not to say that building relationships is easy. There were obstacles. There still are.

*Eric Loftsgard*        *Ken Ekstrom*

## Ezra Is the Teacher

While relationship-building is a natural part of the Nicaraguan culture, investing in the time to build relationships sometimes has been a struggle for some of the North American partners.

"In Latin America, everything is done on the basis of trust that develops during a relationship," said Ken Ekstrom, a former Nicaragua country director for Food for the Hungry, and one of the founders of the center. "North Americans trust until they have reason not to. Latin Americans trust after you have given them a reason to do so. In working [to help Nicaraguans recover from Hurricane Mitch in 1998] we moved quickly because of the relationships we had. Sometimes we were betrayed. But relationships were important to have in place and they made our world go around.

"Part of relationships is that it can take a long time to find who you can trust. Therefore, development work takes a long time. In the first two to three years, you are just building relationships," Ken added.

That's right. Lesson one for the North American partners was to patiently build relationships. In lesson two, North American partners learned that Nicaraguans had to take the leadership role in their own transformation. That was the reasoning behind the creation of the Ezra team.

Ezra, in the Old Testament book that carries his name, was a member of a Jewish family of priests who helped lead the Israelites to rebuild their community after their return to Jerusalem from exile in Babylon. Nehemiah was the builder, and Ezra was the teacher.

From the beginning, the Nehemiah Center founders believed that training should be done by Nicaraguans. Only Nicaraguans could teach biblical worldview in a way that was relevant in Nicaraguan culture. In addition, one of the Nehemiah Center's goals was to develop Nicaraguan leadership. Nicaraguans needed to see other Nicaraguans—not North Americans—in leadership roles. So, already in 1999, the international agencies began assembling the Ezra team of Nicaraguan leaders who would come to be the hub of

Submitted photo

*Róger Pavón, an Ezra team member, provides training in Boaco.*

*Joel Huyser*

what is now the Nehemiah Center.

The native Nicaraguans who make up the Ezra team are equipped to be the trainers. Most often, these people have been receivers of transformation—that is, they have been touched, like Pastor Tomás Ruiz (see Chapter 1), by God to an extent that led them to change their own lives. As they continued their transformation journey, they decided to help others as well.

"It was one of the good ideas of the founders that the foreigners would not be trainers or do follow-up," said Daniel Aragón, a Nicaraguan who was heavily involved in the Nehemiah Center's efforts to improve education. "Instead they would train a group to be in charge of these trainings. This is important because we know the culture and could establish links and agreements without people expecting more. Every time a foreigner is in charge, people think they will help you with everything . . . From the beginning, it has been clear we are a training center. We train and have shown the special value of training for nationals and for organizations."

The truth is that many leaders of the Nicaraguan schools with whom Daniel has worked would see "green" when someone from North America came into their community. That is, they expected handouts from North Americans. But Daniel and other Ezra team members could enter communities with the offer of training, nothing more. "We may tell them we know (North American) partners who want to invest in a project," Daniel continued. "We discuss, and sometimes we say the project is okay but the first benefit they must receive is training. They must be trained in biblical worldview and in transformational development. A saying we have here is, 'Don't pour money into a pocket with a hole.'"

While the Nehemiah Center wants to avoid raising expectations for handouts, there are many other reasons its leaders seek Nicaraguans as trainers. Joel Huyser, one of the founders, recalled an important lesson he heard when veteran missionaries held a conference at a Baptist school in the Nicaraguan city of Masaya. "We did an evaluation afterwards. One of the things that blew me away was that the predominant evaluation comment was this: 'Next time, bring someone who can speak Spanish.' These people [the teachers/leaders] had been in Latin America thirty-plus years! With time, I realized that what the people in Masaya were talking about was not the language as such but the cultural ways of expressing things."

Another example: Daniel Aragón first went to the Dominican Republic six or seven years ago to give a conference on worldview. Joel recalled that after the conference, "They came up to him and said, 'Now we finally understand what the missionaries have been trying to teach us all these years.'

"We may know the language, but we don't know the culture like those who have grown up in it—no matter how many years we live in another country. The thought structure I use is a North

AT A GLANCE

## The Nehemiah Center

History
- Founded in 1999 as a catalyst for Christ-centered leadership in church and society
- Working together, with a shared vision on a joint campus, are:
  - International missionaries and local Christian leaders
  - Community development and church development agencies
  - Volunteers and paid staff members

They are seeking to foster transformation in:
- Marriages
- Families
- Churches
- Schools
- Businesses
- Arts and media
- Local neighborhoods and communities
- Societal structures
- Global relationships in the body of Christ

The Campus
An 8.7-acre campus in southwestern Managua in an area called Nejapa off the old León Highway at KM 10
- 6 acres for NCA Nejapa—a daughter school of the Nicaragua Christian Academy. NCA Nejapa uses Spanish as the primary language with English taught as part of its core curriculum
- 2.7 acres for Nehemiah Center, including living and eating facilities for volunteers

International Partners (More information about the international partners can be found in Appendix A.)
- Caribbean Ministries Association
- Christian Reformed World Missions
- Christian Reformed World Relief Committee
- EduDeo
- Food for the Hungry
- Global CHE Enterprises
- Missionary Ventures International
- Partners Worldwide
- Worldwide Christian Schools

American structure," Joel said. "Leadership training and teaching need to be done by Nicaraguans and interpreted by them. Ultimately, we want to raise up Nicaraguan leadership, not North American leadership."

That is not to say, however, that the Nehemiah Center building was created to be a training center. "The goal is to provide as much training as possible where people live—in their own environments—facilitating their ownership of the process and their own transformations," said Eric Loftsgard. "By design, ninety-five percent of the trainings occur at their own schools, churches, and businesses. We don't want to create disciples of the Nehemiah Center. We are here to accompany and walk with people."

How are the Ezra team members—these agents of transformation—chosen? The Ezra team members have been more identified and empowered than recruited. In other words, they were people who already were on their own paths of transformation. In many ways, the Nehemiah Center just gave them a bigger and better platform to do what they were already doing.

Today, many of those leading the charge for transformation are former or current Ezra team members—people like Henry Cruz, who works to strengthen healthy churches; Róger Pavón, who leads the center's community development efforts; Hultner Estrada and Roberto Armas who equip churches to reach youth at risk; Luz López, a psychologist who has shaped the center's healthy marriage training and who now serves as coordinator of the Ezra team; and Daniel Aragón, a man who once considered himself an atheist and who now champions Christian schools. There will be more about these trainers and their work in subsequent chapters.

North Americans know that it is often easier to work where the expectations are clear, where the route is straight and wide, and where words like "consensus-building" and "partnering" are banned. And, it is true, the path to success hasn't always been a clear one for the Nehemiah Center. There have been failures. There have been times when people chosen to lead programs didn't understand the Nehemiah Center's vision or couldn't navigate the murky areas of "consensus-building" or couldn't grasp the idea that the Nehemiah Center is a community, an agent of transformation, not a funding source. Just that sort of misunderstanding concerning handouts brought about an impasse for a business program launched several years ago.

*Kim Freidah Brown*

When to lead, when to follow, when to help, when to learn, when to watch others struggle—these issues aren't as black-and-white in reality as they may seem on paper. And they surely aren't irrelevant. The Nicaraguans and the North Americans wrestle with these questions sometimes daily. These tensions are examined in Chapter 10.

"Here at the Nehemiah Center, the [cross-cultural] relationship is healthy," said Kim. "We have to work on it and it is not easy, but we have created relationships that are healthy. "

FROM CAROL'S JOURNAL

## *Home Territory with a Twist*

It's our second Sunday morning at Verbo Christian Church in Managua, a worship service more energetic than last week's. In the front row, a man in a lime shirt dances to the fast beat. A woman swirls aloft a long and graceful scarf.

I clumsily clap and move to the unfamiliar rhythms. But, when the message begins, I enter home territory for a Kuyperian Calvinist. The Guatemalan guest preacher, James Janckoviak, describes two kinds of Christians: 1) Believers, waiting for Christ's return with folded arms and 2) Disciples, one hundred percent committed to doing Christ's work until he returns. However, this home territory has a twist.

James tells us about the organic farm he had twenty-five years ago. "I loved that farm. It was my project."

Wanting to serve God, he tried donating fourteen acres for a Christian conference center, but that fell flat. A church elder said, "You want to serve God? Sell your farm. You are married to it!"

He sold his farm for double what he had paid for it.

His church treasurer called on him. "You sold your farm?"

"Yes . . ."

The treasurer cited Acts 2 and said he should give it back to Jesus. James started to sweat. The whole thing?

Two weeks passed. James sat in the back pew of church. He didn't hear what the pastor was saying because he was having his own conversation with God. "Lord, I'll give you a tithe. All of it would be a lot of money."

God was silent.

"Lord, I'll give you a tithe AND an offering." Still silence.

He bargained upwards. Twenty, thirty, forty . . . to one hundred percent.

And at one hundred percent, he heard, "No, not one hundred percent."

"Oh, what a good Lord, I have!" he thought.

He pauses for the congregation to stop laughing and continues.

God added, "I don't want one hundred percent of your money but one hundred percent of you. That includes your money, your wife, your past, your future . . . your all."

He answered, "Lord, I don't want to become a fanatic. I really hope you are coming soon!"

Later, James challenged the congregation: anyone wanting to commit all to Jesus today is asked to come forward. This isn't a commitment to be only a believer, but to be a disciple—to work instead of sitting with arms folded, waiting for the coming of Christ.

During a prayer, these members file before him and he places his hand briefly on each head.

At lunch following the service, I ask two students from a Kuyperian-Calvinist campus if they see differences between the Central American biblical worldview and the one on their North American campus. "I think on campus there is more talk and less action," one of them answers.

And from what I've seen both on Nicaraguan streets and in its sanctuaries, I couldn't agree more.

## Sharing a Biblical Worldview

The centerpiece of all training done by the Nehemiah Center is biblical worldview.

In *Discipling Nations,* the seminal study on worldview for many of those associated with the Nehemiah Center, author Darrow Miller said a worldview is "a set of assumptions, held consciously or unconsciously, about the basic make-up of the world and how the world works."

He said worldview is the set of "glasses we use to view the world." Added Darryl Mortensen, one of the Nehemiah Center's founders: "It is our outlook and perspective on what life is about, on what it means to be human and the purpose of life. Worldview is important because it affects all our relationships: with God, with man, and with creation.

"Biblical worldview says that we are made in God's image and for mutual work with God to shape history and to reconcile all things to himself. In fact, the Great Commission of Matthew 28:18-20[1] makes it clear that all authority in heaven and earth was given to Jesus, and it is out of this power and authority that we as Christians are to disciple all nations. Discipleship is development of people and nations as God intended them to be! What intrigues me about this passage is that it states *nations* and not individuals."[2]

For some, biblical worldview is a new concept. For others, it's a concept understood by the mind, but not the heart. For just about everyone, it is evolving.

"I was introduced to it a year at Regent College, a seminary-level school in British Columbia," said Ken Ekstrom. "They held that there is no separation between clergy and laity. God calls us to all vocations. Then for four years in Guatemala I worked with the Mennonite Central Committee during guerilla warfare, and the year at Regent was very applicable. I saw the effect of worldview, worked with Darrow Miller, and this deepened my biblical worldview."

Gently, and each on their own individual terms, the people who have gravitated toward the Nehemiah Center are becoming more responsive to biblical worldview, exploring it, consuming it, taking it as their own. To understand more how this affects the work at the Nehemiah Center, perhaps it would help to understand other worldviews.

## Conflicting Worldviews

Nicaragua and North America have very different prevailing worldviews, neither of them

---

[1]"Jesus came and told his disciples, 'I have been given all authority in heaven and on earth. Therefore, go and make disciples of all the nations, baptizing them in the name of the Father and the Son and the Holy Spirit. Teach these new disciples to obey all the commands I have given you. And be sure of this: I am with you always, even to the end of the age.'"

[2]"Biblical Worldview in Community Development," Lesson 2 of a 17-lesson community development course taught by Darryl Mortensen to Nicaraguan partner organizations.

purely biblical. North American Christians are influenced by a cultural heritage of secular materialism and individualism.

Nicaraguan Christians—like many other Latin Americans—have been impacted by the historical religions of the area and the version of Catholicism that came with the Spanish conquistadores starting in the early sixteenth century. To some extent—greater and lesser extents in some areas—there is a version of syncretism in Nicaragua in which some of the beliefs of the indigenous people have merged with the Catholicism.

*Francisco Gutiérrez and his wife, Alicia Reyes*

Nehemiah Center board member and physician Francisco Gutiérrez offered examples of Latin American syncretism. "There are villages in which people believe in God and at the same time request saints for miracles. If the saint 'does a miracle,' they take the saint's image to a big party. If the miracle doesn't happen, they remove the clothes from the image, hit him, and turn his face toward the wall until the miracle happens."

The Moravian churches, established by missionaries from Germany, carry another example of syncretism. This church got its start in Nicaragua about 1830 along the east side, along the Atlantic side, where the indigenous Miskito people lived. The Miskitos had many gods; the biggest and most powerful one was Dawan. "When the Bible was translated into Miskito, instead of using God or Jehovah, they used [the name of] Dawan," said Francisco. "They [the Miskitos] embraced the religion but did not leave their own beliefs, but made it a mixture of the two. They believe if you are in the river you can go from one world to another through the river . . .

"Even within the evangelical church, there are beliefs in witches and bad luck. And some evangelical churches focus only within their church, not outside of it.

"Everyone interprets the world through filters they have in their own minds," said Francisco.

*Alma Hernández*

For some Nicaraguans, their worldview has been created and dominated by the economic difficulties of their daily lives. Fatalism is their guiding belief.

"Nicaraguans have no hope and no fallback plan if something goes wrong. They don't believe a change of government will result in any change for them. It will just be more of the same. Many have small worlds," said Alma Hernández, a Nicaraguan staff member at the Nehemiah Center. "We need people to help them see possibilities."

Consider the worldview of the rural, evangelical churches. Eric Loftsgard described Pastor Tomás Ruiz as the perfect example of a pastor of such a church. These pastors often teach that only "spiritual" things are important and that the areas of education, work, and politics are "worldly." With minimal education and no theological training, many have learned to pastor by oral tradition, and the message sometimes becomes warped. Many only know how to preach about a condemning and punishing God. "God is still distant and unreachable, an angry masculine figure, out to punish you," Eric said.

In some of these rural churches, preaching takes on a legalistic, condescending message. "Churches are even laid out as temples. That's one of the reasons why you have to come to church six nights per week and twice on Sunday—because that is where God is. Some believe his spirit is only in that building," said Eric.

Some churches even have a curtain near the podium that represents the curtain in the Jewish temple. "Some pastors view it as the Holy of Holies, and only certain people can go up there," according to Eric. And, following the rules is essential. "You get saved and you must adhere to all the rules. There are strong rules about women's dress. You're heavily judged if you miss a meeting night. And there is very little or no outreach to the community [except] during an evangelistic preaching campaign [where the message is] 'repent or you are going to hell.' "

Eric believes the transformation in Tomás Ruiz has come about largely because of the time Tomás spent reading, pondering, and discussing what must have been new revelations to him in *Discipling Nations.*

For months, Eric led a regular breakfast meeting studying the book with Nicaraguan pastors including Tomás. "We went through it very painstakingly and slowly; this isn't a reading culture," recalled Eric. "Essentially when we got together you had to go through all the high points as a group because they didn't read it or comprehend it on their own. This went on for months and months. It took a year to get through this book, but Tomás was very faithful.

"He is a completely different person than he was eleven years ago."

## Denominational Differences

Besides conflicting worldviews, there are denominational differences that challenge relationship building.

There are more than one hundred different denominations in the country. While some churches are independent, many are part of a formal denomination. These include, in part:

- Catholics. The numbers cited by various sources vary, but clearly well over half of the country's residents still consider themselves at least nominally Catholic.
- Moravians. Almost all are located in the sparsely populated eastern part of the country.
- Baptist churches, with many variations. The churches in the Central American denomination

## Sent with a Catholic Prayer

Living in Grand Rapids, Michigan, Joel and Jeannie Huyser accepted a position in November 1994 to serve in Nicaragua. They, of course, needed to sell their home. Before their real estate agent had even put up a sign, the agent called with someone who wanted to look at the house. Joel agreed, even though Jeannie hadn't had the chance to clean it up and was angry when she learned of the visitors. "The couple came, looked for ten minutes, and asked our price. I told them. They accepted and bought it. That was God's confirmation in our lives," Joel said.

But there was more that God was telling them. The buyers were charismatic Catholics who had moved to Grand Rapids specifically to be part of a charismatic parish. The couple invited the Huysers to their church on a Sunday morning. Their priest announced during mass that the Huysers were there and would soon be serving as missionaries. " 'We want to pray for them,' the priest said. And he called us forward to pray for us," Joel recalled.

"The significance of that came later: Once we came to Latin America, we could sense such an incredible divide between the Protestant and Catholic churches. In Latin America, most evangelicals cannot accept that a Catholic can truly be a Christian. That prayer was a strong word from the Lord we were not to go that route. Catholics were praying for our mission to a Catholic country."

are closely related to the Baptists.
- Pentecostal churches, which include the Assembly of God and the Church of God. They make up the majority of Protestant churches.
- Mennonite churches.
- Church of Nazarene.
- Independent and emerging churches.

These independent churches are congregations that are not part of an historical denomination. In some cases, two or more independent churches have banded together. In other cases, these churches start daughter churches that band together to form an association of churches.

According to Daniel Boniche, prior to 1972 there simply were no relationships among denominations. But when a devastating earthquake hit Managua just before Christmas that year, 700,000 people had to be evacuated from the capital. As these people sought out churches in new cities, there was a *mezcla* (mixing) of the denominations, resulting in better relationships among them. The high level of economic and physical need at that time also helped improve relationships.

Politically, the situation was complex as well. During the 1980s, *Consejo de Iglesias Pro-Alianza Denominacional* (CEPAD), a group of evangelical pastors and churches formed in the aftermath of the 1972 Managua earthquake, tended to support the Sandinista government while another organization of pastors and churches, *Consejo Nacional de Pastores Evangelicos de Nicaragua* (CNPEN), tended to oppose the government. The political divisiveness in the country—clearly intense at times—was apparent not just between denominations, but often within denominations, even within individual churches and individual families.

The history of these churches is one of distrust; quite simply, they often refused to talk to one another. This is the environment entered by the Nehemiah Center.

Somehow, despite the differences, the Nehemiah Center has forged relationships. The Ezra team comes from many different denominations, and the pastoral couples in the local networks come from different denominations. The differences aren't as important as the similarities. "We all agree that we are not going to talk about our areas of difference. Tongues, baptism, eschatology—we don't talk about them. We talk about the things we agree on," said Darryl Mortensen.

---

FROM CAROL'S JOURNAL

### *Stretched between Cultures*

Nicaraguan Jairo Solano is my driver and translator for several interviews in León. As he turns north out of Managua, I ask about his impeccable English. He tells me he lived in the United States from 2000 to 2009 with his wife, Kelly, a U.S. citizen.

Picturing a wishbone sort of life straddling two distant-from-each-other cultures, I ask him about his life in a different culture, and in his own.

Jairo had a Nicaraguan business degree, but at first could only land a house-painting job in the United States. Embarrassed, he invented fake jobs to tell his Nicaraguan friends and family. "In Nicaragua," he says, "your work identifies who you are." Educated jobs earn respect; manual labor does not. When he confessed, his mother was sad about his manual labor, even though he told her he was glad to have the job.

Nicaraguans worry less about the future than North Americans, he says. Most don't think about retirement funds. His father, for example, at sixty-two, closed his small hardware store, keeping only a little inventory to prevent boredom. "He spends his time reading the Bible and other books. He has a laid-back mentality about the future."

Jairo laughs, then says this laid-back attitude is not true of very rich Nicaraguans. They are more like North Americans. His sixty-seven-year-old uncle owns eight thousand acres and works fifty to sixty hours per week. "He is no longer a Christian. He worries about money—and he is rich. He doesn't have God—he has all this money!"

When Jairo returned to Nicaragua in 2009, he became a Food for the Hungry coordinator for North American service-and-learning teams. He says that North American and Nicaraguan construction processes and standards sometimes clash. "Both nationalities think they have the right way of doing things."

He adds, "I know both cultures. I can be a link that connects, for a better result."

Ninety minutes later, as we enter León, I realize Jairo is not uncomfortable straddling two cultures after all. No, he is a builder of bridges.

I'd like to be a bridge-builder, too.

"The Nehemiah Center is non-threatening," Darryl added. "We teach that Christians need to get along and if we don't we will lose.

"I originally was Presbyterian, but in Guam, I became part of the Faith Presbyterian Reformed Church not knowing that it was part of the Christian Reformed Church. Can you imagine that? And when I applied at CRWRC [Christian Reformed World Relief Committee], they teased me about that."

## Through a Builder's Eyes

Hands crossed behind his head, leaning back in his chair, Eric Loftsgard planned to explain the architecture of the open-air hallway and quadrangle of offices that make up the Nehemiah Center. But first, he talked about the reconstruction inside his own heart.

When he arrived in Nicaragua in August 1998 with Missionary Ventures International, Eric continued to see himself as a contractor. He knew how to lead projects; he knew how to get projects done within a budget.

"I am a builder—that's God's gift to me." He expected that God planned for him to use his gift.

That wasn't God's plan.

Eric discovered he had much to learn before he could build. The culture was completely opposite to his nature. He was task-oriented; Nicaraguans were relationship-oriented. He counted time by minutes; they counted it by events. He measured their

*Eric Loftsgard makes a point.*

poverty materially; they measured their lives through relationships. He saw a need to help all Nicaraguans; many Nicaraguan churches were focused only on themselves and their own needs.

In addition to these disconnects, he found himself in the middle of Hurricane Mitch disaster relief just months after he arrived. Abundant aid poured into the country. He handed out food and clothes and supplies and helped rebuild, all the while wondering if he was doing the right thing. He saw the long-term dependency that was being created.

"I thought I came to Nicaragua to build buildings, thinking I would literally build the kingdom via church and school buildings. I learned fairly quickly, within the first two years, that building has very little to do with the big picture. I needed to step back and try to grasp the big picture. In trying to transform people, building a building in a timely fashion was only about five percent of the equation.

"My priorities were mixed up . . . With my North American background and worldview, I was actually opposed to the values and objectives we were trying to achieve in these people and in their communities! It was a huge re-evaluation for me personally. I found out how much of me personally and my culture got in the way, and I couldn't justify it biblically.

"Our North American values have to be re-prioritized and rechecked within ourselves before we can do that in others. We're all on a transformation journey. We are all being transformed and have to evaluate our worldview."

As Eric hunted for answers, he read more books in his first years in Nicaragua than he had in the previous thirty. He talked about his dilemmas with other missionaries who attended a roundtable that Darryl Mortensen and Ken Ekstrom had begun. Gradually, he came to see that his job was working with Nicaraguan people, not giving to them. He saw the individualism and materialism of his North American mindset, even though he was a Christian. "I saw that I wasn't going to change a whole Nicaraguan culture [and shouldn't]. I was going to have to do some changing myself."

Eric has become a man on a mission of two-way transformation: helping to transform Nicaraguans and North Americans—along with himself—so that both cultures are more in keeping with a biblical worldview.

He turned his attention back to the building around him, gesturing at the surrounding space. "All offices face the hall and usually have open doors. Everyone sees everyone coming and going. I'll pass seven other offices and talk to three or four people before I get where I am going. There are more ideas exchanged in that informal way than any meeting you could organize. That's why there are tables and chairs in the hallway for people to relate informally."

Words spilled in a torrent as he pointed to other features—the cistern underneath that collects water to irrigate the center's courtyard, the tree he saved along with the rest of the natural foliage, and the high, continuous windows on the offices.

Eric called attention to the wrought iron work in the doors and windows, made by the students in the vocational school started by Tomás Ruiz in Los Brasiles—a vocational school that now has a branch on the Nehemiah Center campus.

He talked about the openness that allows for cross ventilation and cultural differences. "The two maladies in this environment are heat and dust. So, if you want a cooler building, you keep it open. It's all about airflow: That's my camp. Nicaraguans are in the other camp: It's about cleanliness. They seal everything up and keep the dust out and cook themselves. There needed to be a balance." Eric originally designed the building so that each room had top-of-the wall openings to the quadrangle. But, to keep out dust and leaves, some of those openings were closed in.

"It was a process in which we listened to input from everyone, and worked on consensus. People had differing ideas, but I would never classify it as combative or conflictive. We worked on consensus for everything—room sizes and flow and layout." Both the end product and the process foster community.

"What holds us together is our deeply held shared mission and vision, and if you don't believe that then you can't be a partner. Our mission and vision are the price of admission. You have to believe in the Nehemiah community's three pillars: collaboration, transformation, and biblical worldview."

*A memorial in honor of some of those who died in Hurricane Mitch*

# 03

## Bonding in the Wake of Disaster

*After I arrived in Nicaragua, one of first things Darryl said to me was, "Can we be friends?" By that he meant, can we share our personal lives with each other, ask each other for prayer, and share what we are working on. I believe that question was the first spark for the Nehemiah Center.*

-JOEL HUYSER

It was the sound—a loud, deep, and persistent rumble—that initially caught Abelina Caballero's attention. *A helicopter!* Why would a helicopter be coming to her small Nicaraguan village?

Something inside Abelina warned her that the helicopter probably wasn't good news. For one thing, little good news filtered to her village, just one hundred small houses perched on the side of a defunct volcano in the León province. Secondly, Hurricane Mitch had been hard on them, dropping torrential amounts of rainfall in the past few days.

So, when Abelina ran out of her hut on October 30, 1998, she didn't know what to expect, didn't know why a helicopter needed to visit her village.

What she saw when she ran outside wasn't a helicopter. Instead, she saw a roaring wall of mud thundering down the mountain, wiping out animals, trees, houses. With devastating speed, it surged through El Porvenir, and it buried Abelina waist-deep, crushing three of her ribs and breaking her cheekbones.

When the roar of the mudslide died down, she could hear mud-trapped adults, children, and infants scream and moan and die. Over and over, Abelina tried to calm a nearby child—trapped as she herself was—encouraging the boy to conserve his energy and prevent him from dehydrating.

For two days, the Nicaraguan government dismissed the mudslide as a rumor before finally launching a rescue. The slide had been eighteen kilometers long and, in places, a kilometer deep.

Abelina Caballero

Three days after being buried, Abelina was rescued by helicopter. Following multiple surgeries and a month of hospitalization, she was dismissed to a temporary shelter and began searching for her family. Her daughter and a son had survived. Her husband, a married son, his wife, and three children had not. One year later, she, along with other survivors, relocated to the village of Santa Maria, created for mudslide survivors on ninety acres of donated land.

With variations, Abelina's suffering was replicated thousands of times in thousands of places in Nicaragua. Hard lives became harder.

The devastation wrought by the category 5 hurricane cannot be overstated. Extensive rainfall had essentially stalled over the country. By some estimates, more than fifty inches fell. Abelina's village was on the side of the Casita Volcano. According to the U.S. National Climatic Data Center, the rainfall filled the lake at the crater of the dormant volcano, causing some of its walls to collapse. The resulting mudslide buried at least four villages and eventually covered an area at least ten miles long and five miles wide.

Virtually all of Nicaragua had been affected by the flooding caused by the torrential rainfall. Thousands were dead in the country. Thousands more were missing, and hundreds of thousands were homeless. Roads and bridges were gone, crops were destroyed, animals were killed. Water was contaminated and in short supply, as was food.

It was in the aftermath of these conditions that the Nehemiah Center got its start.

## Praying for Hope

Hurricane Mitch changed more than the Nicaraguan countryside. As Darryl Mortensen, a North American missionary in the country at the time remembered, "Mitch brought us all to our knees, praying together."

Praying with Darryl were Joel Huyser and Ken Ekstrom.

What they didn't know at the time was that their prayers and thoughts would eventually take them not just to a new model for missionary work and collaboration, but also would lead them to transform their own personal thinking and worldview; lead them to cultivate changes in churches, communities, families, health, agriculture, and businesses; and lead them to form a new collaboration called the Nehemiah Center. Their prayers led them to changes that can't be measured with numbers or statistics. How do you measure a transformation in thinking and a transformation in living?

Agriculturalist Darryl Mortensen was the veteran. He started his international journey working for the Peace Corps in Thailand and was a farmer and teacher in Guam (he holds master's and doctorate degrees in agriculture education), before ultimately joining Christian Reformed World Relief Committee (CRWRC). He has been the program consultant or country director for CRWRC in Sierra Leone, Mexico, Honduras, and Nicaragua.

FROM CAROL'S JOURNAL

## *Place of Pain*

Traveling the Managua-to-Chinandega highway with a church team from Burlington, Ontario, Canada, I spot a brown gash in the side of one of the line of volcanoes east of the highway. I learn that gash is our destination: Casita Memorial Park. After twelve years, the devastation from the massive mudslide remains visible, even from a distance.

As we walk toward the visitor center, a guide tells us that even forty days after the slide, the ground underfoot was too soft to support a walker's weight. Roberto Armas, our Nehemiah Center Ezra staff host, tells us he recently took a class of Nicaraguan youth leaders here also. "Hearing testimonies of survivors impacted them—to hear that life is not only joyful, but sometimes painful," he says. From two villages—Rolando Rodríguez and El Porvenir—only forty-five people survived.

"Nicaragua has many places of pain," I think, remembering other stops: downtown Managua, flattened by an earthquake, and *Parque de la Paz* (Peace Park) where half-buried weapons poke from a wall of cement, dirt, and weeds as reminders of recent civil wars.

Yet, hope and beauty grow here, also. Dieffenbachia and poinsettias flourish in this tropical habitat. Trees, too. One team member says he is amazed at the tree size. In just twelve years, trees grew much bigger here than they would have in his Canadian backyard.

Our guide tells us each tree—and there are 2,800 of them—commemorates a person obliterated. Unrecovered, two thousand bodies lie beneath our feet. The eight hundred recovered bodies lie in a mass grave under the stone monument in front of us.

"This is a holy place," he says.

We fall silent, our thoughts with those below. He tells us that each October 30 a memorial service on these grounds commemorates their deaths.

A holy place, indeed.

*Some of the Nehemiah Center team at a 2001 meeting. Left to right, Eric Loftsgard, Darryl Mortensen, Joel Huyser, Manuel Largaespada, Ken Ekstrom, and Juan Granados*

Engineer Ken Ekstrom had arrived in the country in 1994. He worked as a technology developer for the Mennonite Central Committee in Guatemala, then as a mechanical engineer for SunAmp Systems, Inc., in Scottsdale, Arizona, a company involved with solar heating, cooling, and hot water systems. In 1986, he joined Food for the Hungry, Inc., a job that eventually led him to Nicaragua.

Lawyer Joel Huyser was the "new kid on the block," as Ken put it, sent there by Christian Reformed World Missions (CRWM) in 1996. Raised in the small central Iowa town of Sully, Joel's journey to Nicaragua was roundabout. For a brief time in college, he even considered himself an atheist. He obtained his law degree in Colorado, then lived fourteen years in Michigan while raising a family, working in a law firm, and taking an active part in church life. After a year spent learning Spanish in Costa Rica, Joel arrived in Nicaragua in August 1996.

Joel was the newbie, but through Ken and Darryl, his vision grew. "Joel went to a training session that Ken and I were giving. It changed Joel completely," Darryl recalled. "We had twenty to thirty years of development experience. Joel had none. Joel realized what he was doing was wrong and he changed it."

Added Ken: "As he [Joel] got more committed to development work, he started seeing his role as similar to Darryl's for a different audience. It was interesting to see his development. He is a visionary. I was an implementer. Darryl was a mentor."

All the men describe their relationship as complementary. According to Joel, Ken is "one of the smartest people I have ever met in my life. He has a photographic memory. He knows Greek, Hebrew, engineering, accounting, and remembers everything."

And, added Joel, "Darryl became for me and many of us another mentor—the source for much of what all of us learned about the international and later national part of community development."

Together, the characteristics each man brought to the table created an environment for growth.

"Ken is extremely intelligent in technical fields, Joel in the law field," said Darryl. "I have more of a balanced, average intelligence. That's who I am compared to those two guys. If you asked Joel to give you a screwdriver, he would tell you he doesn't drink. With Ken, every time

AT A GLANCE
## *Nicaragua*

Location: Bordered by Honduras on the north, Costa Rica on the south, the Pacific Ocean on the west, and the Caribbean Sea on the east

Geography: Largest country in Central America. Contains the largest freshwater body in Central America: Lake Nicaragua

Capital: Managua

Population: Nearly 6 million people—not quite double the population of the state of Iowa

Land Area: 130,370 sq km (50,309 square miles)—a little smaller than Iowa

Economy: The poorest country in Central America. Population below poverty line: 48 percent (2005 figure)

Brief History:

· Settled as Spanish colony in the 16th century

· Celebrates Independence Day on September 15, a commemoration of the declaration of independence from Spain in 1821

· Ruled by the Somoza family starting in 1936

· Sandinista Revolution ended Somoza rule on July 19, 1979

· Daniel Ortega elected president in 1984

· Violeta Barrios de Chamorro elected president in 1990, Arnoldo Alemán elected in 1996, and Enrique Bolaños in 2001. Ortega re-elected in November 2006

he talks everything goes to numbers because he is an engineer. Eric [Loftsgard] and I were medium on both sides [of the brain]. All four of us together made a very good mix. When you mixed it together it became a powerful entity."

The environment for growth was established. But what exactly would grow?

In these early days, the missionaries were asking a lot of questions of themselves and pretty much anyone who would listen. What was their role? What should be their role? They went beyond asking how true change could happen, to ask deeper questions. What was change? What should it be? Who should it be?

Joel, according to Darryl, initially saw his role as a church developer. Darryl considered himself more of a community developer—taking a community and helping it to get on its feet and go where it wants to go in agriculture, health, literacy, education, housing, and more. In time, Joel sought out something even larger—development of an entire country or society.

As the men were asking these questions, they were joined by others, such as Eric Loftsgard, who came to join in on the discussions after Hurricane Mitch raised similar questions in his mind. Is their work really helping the country? Is massive relief creating dependence?

Another issue they were struggling with was how to transition from relief to development work, now that Mitch was receding into the background. And they saw worldview training as a crucial component of that.

The fact that these missionaries from different agencies and different denominations were asking these questions of each other was unusual. As discussed in the previous chapter, collaboration among missionaries is the exception, not the norm.

Why did they collaborate? Before serving in Nicaragua, Ken had been in Guatemala where there were seven hundred missionaries. Each organization had a score of staff members, but they stayed in their own groups. So what was different this time in Nicaragua?

In part, it was their shared experiences. Many attended worship at the International Chris-

---

## AT A GLANCE
### *Nicaragua Politics*

The history of the Sandinistas and their opposition groups in Nicaragua is a long and complicated one. A brief review may be helpful to understand the Nicaraguan people.

The Sandinistas take their name from Augusto Cesar Sandino, the leader of a rebellion group opposed to U.S. military occupation of the country in the 1920s and early 1930s. Sandino was assassinated by Anastasio Somoza's forces in 1934. The Somoza family then gained control of the country and ruled Nicaragua from 1936 to the revolution in 1979.

The Sandinista National Liberation Front (in Spanish, *Frente Sandinista de Liberacion Nacional* or FSLN) originated in the early 1960s. Throughout the 1970s, the clash between the FSLN and the Somoza government intensified. Censorship and widespread violence was common. In 1979, the FSLN overthrew Somoza, putting its own socialist political party in power.

The Sandinistas created a ruling Junta, or council, made up of five members. This included three Sandinistas (one of them militant Daniel Ortega) and two non-Sandinista members (one of them Violeta Barrios de Chamorro, whose husband, a popular editor of a newspaper, had been assassinated in January 1979, presumably by Somoza sympathizers).

By 1980, conflicts within the Junta were common, and Chamorro resigned. Sandinista opposition groups began to form; these were counter-revolutionaries known as the Contras, financed by the United States during Ronald Reagan's administration. By 1982, the Sandinistas declared an official state of emergency that lasted six years and which curtailed many freedoms. In January 1985, after a much-disputed election, Daniel Ortega took control of the government as president. The United States continued to finance the Contras and enforced an embargo on Nicaragua, and the country's economic problems worsened.

Hoping to end the conflicts, Violeta Barrios de Chamorro was elected president in 1990, defeating Ortega, with a promise to end the military draft and improve the country's economy. Arnoldo Alemán was elected in 1996, and Enrique Bolaños was elected leader of the country in 2001. Ortega ran in all three elections but lost. It wasn't until November 2006 that he was re-elected as the country's leader.

tian Fellowship (ICF), and their children attended Nicaragua Christian Academy (NCA). In part, it was their personalities, their openness, and their willingness to explore their questions. In part, it was because Nicaragua had far fewer missionaries than Guatemala—only a hundred or so evangelical missionaries were in the country. All these reasons played a role in their collaboration.

In short, they needed each other.

## Birth of an Idea

Ken had been influenced by the book *Discipling Nations: The Power of Truth to Transform Cultures*, written by then Food for the Hungry (FH) staffer Darrow Miller and Stan Guthrie. It had convinced Ken of the importance of a biblical worldview—a subject the three men considered essential for Nicaragua, where animism often blended with Christian thought. Ken wanted to organize a Disciple Nations Alliance (DNA) vision conference in Nicaragua. DNA vision conferences, a collaboration between FH and Harvest Foundation, have impacted Christians around the world with their teachings linking worldview, culture, and development. But Ken and his staff were still swamped with hurricane relief work.

He told Joel and Darryl, "My home office is asking me to organize a conference, but in the wake of Mitch, I don't think I can pull it off." They urged him to move ahead with planning it, telling him they would help.

It was at about this same time that a conviction surfaced within Darryl. "It was as if God were saying, 'You guys need to be doing something better than you are doing.'" Darryl had been considering this need for a better way when Ken made his request.

The three set this parameter: the conference should appeal to the full range of Nicaraguan Christians and motivate them to work together in their communities. That alone was unusual. In Nicaragua, it seemed as if the divisions among its people were endless. Charismatics, evangelicals, Pentecostals, and Catholics were sharply divided. And, following years of civil war, many Sandinista (socialist) and non-Sandinista Christians wouldn't speak to each other.

There were also the differences in worldview. Some, as Francisco Gutiérrez described in Chapter 2, held long-standing beliefs that included elements of both Christianity and the animism of the native people.[1] Some, like Pastor Tomás Ruiz in Chapter 1, believed in separation of the church and the world. Many of the Christians who were interested in social change had given up on the church and started their own organizations. The divisions on many fronts were numerous and obvious.

What were these men thinking?

---

[1]Animism is the concept that spirits animate everything, that is, that objects have spirits and the physical world is an illusion. Thus, animists often believe that bad things happen because the spirits are angry; to resolve a crisis, the spirits must be appeased. If the spirits can't be appeased, there is nothing else that can be done.

"Darryl, Joel, and I sometimes joked that if we had been traditional, seminary-trained missionaries, we probably would have never founded such a program or institution," said Ken Ekstrom.

For a church conference site, the men settled on Verbo Christian Church—where Ken and Mary Ann Ekstrom as well as Joel and Jeannie Huyser had been members. The church, as Darryl described it, was a "large, non-threatening, nondenominational church" in Managua. Its pastor, Ricardo Hernández, and several other Managua pastors helped with planning and organization. "Strategically, we chose the most neutral venue we could," said Ken.

The Verbo church was the perfect middle ground. It included some Pentecostal and non-Pentecostal members as well as some Sandinistas and non-Sandinistas.

Joel in particular thought the Verbo location was a good choice because he could see God working already in that church. At the first worship service he attended there, Joel listened to Ricardo preach about the need for Christians to transform all areas of society. "We were not bringing this in for the first time," Joel said. "God had already brought that in."

The planners announced it on the radio, sent letters to churches, and asked people they knew to tell others—this latter method of getting the message out being the most important in this country where relationships govern actions. They invited all Managua-area pastors to a conference on biblical worldview for *all* Christians, regardless of denomination or political party. Some, Eric Loftsgard in particular, became very active in promotion and recruiting people to attend.

From the start, Nicaraguan leaders worked on the team. These early leaders included Manuel Largaespada and his wife, Luz López; Pastor Ricardo Hernández from Verbo; Róger Pavón, formerly president of his denomination's board of directors; Guadalupe Gómez, a Baptist pastor and later president of the Baptist Convention; Francisco Gutiérrez, a Verbo member and a physician who later became director of Christian Medical Action; and Roberto Rojas, then superintendent of the Assembly of God, the largest Protestant denomination in Nicaragua.

"The team also became key people in the Nehemiah Center movement. It is amazing how God throughout our history has brought us the right people," said Joel. "God allowed certain relationships to be formed and in the right moment those people were used."

As team members planned, they hoped maybe a few dozen pastors would attend. When the conference opened in June 1999, two hundred people walked through the Verbo church doors, accepted their three-ring binders of resources for the weekend, and seated themselves on metal folding chairs at the white plastic tables in the open Verbo sanctuary.

Still not speaking to each other, the Sandinistas and non-Sandinistas sat on opposite sides of the sanctuary. The pastors, many wearing *guayabera* (embroidered dress shirts), sat around the white tables, informally grouping themselves by denomination. An uncomfortable mood hung in the air.

The only sense of "togetherness" for this bunch was that they were in the same dark cinder-blocked room, exhaust fans offering the only comfort to the heat that wasn't just physical.

It would take powerful words to bridge these differences.

## Developing a Common Language

Submitted photo

*Darrow Miller teaches at a March 2000 worldview conference at Verbo church.*

During the three-day conference, the participants spent a lot of time studying Scripture, and a lot of time working out issues for themselves.

Scripture tells us that Christians should love God and neighbor. The participants were asked then, "Whom should you love?" They were forced to find the answers themselves.

Many pastors had been preaching that if Nicaraguans don't have to work, that is good. Again, Scripture was brought out, and questions were asked. Often, the conference broke up into teams to consider questions. Often they were asked to write down their answers, sometimes on a board, then read them aloud.

"Without our telling them the answers, they learned," said Ken. "We didn't say anything as outsiders." It was a technique that helped these pastors realize they had to pull together, especially post-Mitch.

A Spanish version of the first chapter of Darrow Miller's book that had so influenced the organizers was included in the notebooks the participants received.

The Managua-area pastors went home at night. Others, who traveled in for the conference, stayed with family or friends. Lunch was catered in. Singing was part of the meetings. Arturo Cubas, a Bolivian native then working for FH in Guatemala, was a speaker. Luis Sena from the Dominican Republic was another speaker. "If a gringo talked, they would not even listen," Ken said. "At the end of his [Sena's] speech, a Sandinista friend asked for a copy of it. I knew then that the message was getting through."

"By the end of three days they were talking to each other. I watched the leaders who had not spoken to each other for ten years begin to talk," Darryl recalled with wonder. "By the end of the conference, we were surprised, really surprised. That opened the door. They actually voted for another conference on biblical worldview."

Also as a result, change, like the change for Tomás Ruiz, began to happen. A survey done afterward found that a significant number had followed up on a conference recommendation to start seed projects—small community projects that incorporate both the Word and deed and that are done completely with the resources of the local church.

"What we sensed was that the idea of a kingdom theology gave people a language and a framework in which they could dialog and eventually work beyond these differences," said Joel.

But the Nicaraguans were not the only people affected. Darryl confessed, "It changed my life. I thought I knew something about biblical worldview, but I was on the short end of the stick."

## Missionary Transformations

As a result of the Verbo conference and other conferences, and through their discussions with each other, all the North American planners and Nicaraguan leaders were going through a transformation—being made new in their vision of their Christian responsibility in God's world.

### Darryl Mortensen

*Darryl Mortensen*

"I worked for CRWRC for twenty years and overseas twenty-eight years, and it was the most exciting, beautiful, God-centered thing that ever happened to me. It was an experience that had never happened to me before," said Darryl about the conference.

"I was sixty years old when I really began to understand biblical worldview. I asked God why he waited so long to make it so clear to me. I got to spend the next five years on that, and it became a major part of what I was doing. I told CRWRC we needed to focus on biblical worldview. Joel understood it better than I did. I'm seventy-two now. I wish I were forty and I knew what I knew when I left Nicaragua. But by that time I had been in the field forty years; I was exhausted. I was really tired."

### Joel Huyser

*Joel Huyser*

As a successful trial lawyer who considers the theories and philosophies behind actions, Joel has often been the impetus for the Nehemiah Center's collaboration. Intensely focused, Joel is a visionary. Initially, he was brought into the country to work as the leadership developer under Christian Reformed World Missions—essentially to help strengthen the small Christian Reformed churches that had been planted after the 1972 earthquake that had destroyed Managua.

As biblical worldview became a more important concept, and as the international organizations started working together, Joel could see more opportunities.

"After the 1999 conference, we all had the idea we needed to follow up from the conference and spread some things taught at that time further," said Joel. Introducing biblical worldview in the context of improving marriages and families was a first step. Christian schools seemed to be the next appropriate step. Then, business development, community development, youth at risk, arts and media. Making changes, bringing the concepts of biblical worldview into all these areas could transform lives.

"One of my strong beliefs and arguments was that we [as foreigners] should stay in the background as far as possible and find local Nicaraguan leaders to do the front-line training," said Joel. "This was something I had learned from Darryl and his experience in community development. That became the beginning of the Ezra team. We would work behind the scenes, have lots of deep discussions, and do some formal training."

The nationals originally were attracted to the Nehemiah Center because it gave them a platform to do what they were already committed to do. "However, many of them did not have the complete understanding of biblical worldview," said Joel. "But in a short time they had all internalized the vision.

"The structure has been a developmental process, but is near to what I envisioned in the beginning: that the core would be the Nicaraguan leadership in the Ezra team complemented by a Nicaraguan support staff that would serve both Ezra and the collaborating international agencies. The work of the Nehemiah Center continues as long as there is funding for what it is doing," he added.

"I think if the Nicaraguan government were to order North Americans to leave tomorrow, very little would change as long as we can fund it. The international organizations are all replaceable. I see the Nehemiah Center continuing in the future as long as the Ezra team can attract other national and international collaborators."

### Ken Ekstrom

*Ken Ekstrom*

"The response to the 1999 conference proved far beyond what we had planned—let alone what we would have been able to do by human means alone," said Ken. The biblical basis of the material presented at that conference, and really from the very beginning of the organizations' work in the country, was critical. "When FH started its leadership training program in 1995, the Nicaraguan participants were very skeptical until they saw that the teaching was biblically based and in many cases straight from the Bible," said Ken. The reasons for this were obvious in a country racked by division. "It was important that we did not have a political or denominational agenda."

Back late in 1995, Ken, working for Food for the Hungry, along with CRWRC representative Roland Hoksbergen, started a monthly roundtable discussion group for expatriate Chris-

## A Suspected Contra

The political conflict between the Sandinistas and their enemies is interwoven throughout the personal lives of most Nicaraguans. Ricardo Hernández, for instance, used counterfeit papers–identifying himself as Nicaraguan although he had been born in El Salvador–during his first years in the country. When he became a Christian, he wanted to tell the truth and decided to leave Puerto Cabezas, a community on Nicaragua's eastern coast, for Managua, where he could correct his records.

His timing couldn't have been worse. In 1982, the Sandinistas and the Contras were fighting hard along the northern border of Nicaragua near Puerto Cabezas. He registered his name three days in advance for a flight to Managua as required–and was immediately suspected of being a Contra. He was sent to Managua–to be put in jail. After a month in jail, Ricardo was able to prove his El Salvadoran citizenship and was released, proper paperwork in hand.

Although legally exempted from military duty, he–like all Managua residents–was expected to participate in a civil defense committee. His task was to make rounds guarding the neighborhood and to help dig trenches as shelters from the potential aerial bombing by the United States. He and ten other members of his Verbo church were trained in first aid as part of the civil defense program. Ricardo was living in the Verbo sanctuary at this time, employed as the church's janitor.

tians working in Nicaragua—a.k.a. "the dumb gringos support group." This roundtable laid the foundation for the collaborative efforts that later became the Nehemiah Center.

"All three of the founding agencies were committed—at least in theory and to a large degree in practice—to a biblical worldview and to ministry to the whole person," said Ken. "As time went on and we worked together, the practice became even more aligned with the theory."

That commitment, along with the connection many felt to each other personally, led the agencies to reach beyond their boundaries. "All three founding agencies had mandates to assist in the building up of the programs of local groups rather than developing themselves as institutions," added Ken. "This allowed them to systematically and openly reach out across institutional and denominational lines. Even Christian Reformed World Missions [which has an evangelism and discipleship focus] had the freedom to work with others, especially in its partnership with CRWRC.

"Sometimes people have asked me how they can duplicate the Nehemiah Center. I say you can't. If all the factors are not working together and God is not in it, it won't happen. A lot more happened at the first conference than we planned. God's hand was obvious. However, the principles of the Nehemiah Center, including collaborative effort, can be useful to others."

*Pastor Ricardo Hernández*

Ricardo Hernández, the pastor of the Verbo church where that first biblical worldview conference was held, was born in El Salvador into a family of fifteen children. When

*Ricardo
Hernández*

he was fifteen, he decided his family didn't need or care for him, and he took his clothes, put them in a bag, and started walking.

"I didn't know where I was going, but I didn't care. Sometimes I walked twenty-five to thirty kilometers per day. Sometimes I slept on the porch of a house and in the morning woke and went again. And that is how I arrived at the border of Honduras."

He got into a small boat and crossed the Gulf of Fonseca into Nicaragua. He swung a machete cutting sugar cane, or picked cotton, earning enough to eat. Six years passed. Then someone invited him to an evangelical church—a place he thought he would never enter, especially considering his brother was a Catholic priest. A month later, Ricardo went back to the church. "God spoke to me and said 'you are tired and laden.' I felt very special about that, and I went to the front and prayed. That day something happened in me. I felt the forgiveness from God totally. I felt that God told me . . . 'I will help you,' and with that I started my Christian life."

Soon, Ricardo joined the newly formed Verbo church. He cleaned toilets and got the church ready for people. Later, he became a deacon; later still, an elder; and in 1991, he became pastor.

After the Verbo conference, he became more involved with the work of the Nehemiah Center. "It is a special way to work together because we are all different denominations and different people and sit together to talk about how to grow the whole society integrally.

"When I began to be a Christian, I was thinking only of the local church, and I was thinking this is all," said Ricardo. "But when I listened about biblical worldview I thought, okay, God established families and churches and governments and businesses. I began to understand that all of this is the kingdom of God and you are in the kingdom in each of these."

Admittedly reluctant to have his church host that first conference, Ricardo has served for several terms as board president for the Nehemiah Center. "This worldview helps me to see more opportunities to preach the gospel, more opportunities to help people see the kingdom. It is not only in the local church . . . I am growing yet." After that first conference, Ricardo took the message to other pastors. "We must amplify the mission of the gospel. That was my topic."

### Francisco Gutiérrez

*Francisco
Gutiérrez*

Born into a Catholic family, Francisco Gutiérrez only occasionally went to church as he was growing up. Later, when he got to know Alicia (who later became his wife), he became interested in her evangelical church, and started reading the Bible. When an armed movement in his hometown forced his family into the country, Alicia's church came to this rural area to preach. "This is where I learned the Gospel and realized my need for Jesus and when I accepted Jesus,"

Francisco said.

Francisco can see the impact biblical worldview and the Nehemiah Center have made in his country and in his own ministry as a physician and former director of *Accion Medica Cristiana* (Christian Medical Action). "When you share values with other organizations and when you have the same passion and when you consider that your work is a ministry, then when you do your work, you do it with quality. You don't get tired of it because it is your passion," said Francisco, who now is president of the Nehemiah Center board. "I believe we have grown because of being integrated with the Nehemiah Center. Understand, all the impact the Nehemiah Center has done is impossible for me to explain or see because I have just been a small part of it on the board of directors.

"At the Nehemiah Center, I have not only received, but I have also given. This is not pride. In all my work, I have also given to the work of the Nehemiah Center. And many of my ideas have been accepted and implemented and that helps me to continue to be filled with passion for my own ministry."

## From Sharing Ideas to Sharing Space

Because of Hurricane Mitch, Food for the Hungry had expanded greatly and had rented a house. But after the conference, response to Mitch was winding down and the organization didn't need the house. At the same time that FH was closing its large relief office, the CRWRC and the CRWM were looking for new offices. In July 1999, the agencies decided to jointly rent a new office and share both space and support staff. The three organizations rented a house, crowding into a main floor office space. Short-term volunteers were housed in the dank basement of the house.

Meanwhile, they continued to talk, not just Ken, Darryl, and Joel, but others, too. Eric Loftsgard with Missionary Ventures, Pastor Ricardo Hernández with the Verbo church, and others. Manuel Largaespada and Luz López, psychologists who had been involved since the planning of the 1999 conference, suggested introducing biblical worldview in the context of improving marriages and families.

And, they continued to ask questions. Continued to talk about collaboration. Continued to welcome differences while making connections centered on biblical worldview.

Soon, they discovered they needed a name for this unorganized umbrella group that they had become. They chose "Nehemiah Center" after the prophet Nehemiah who rebuilt the walls surrounding Jerusalem so that it could again be a vibrant and healthy and safe city.

In 2002, the Nehemiah Center incorporated, and in 2007, moved to its current home.

It was, and still is, a collaboration of differences centered on serving God through a biblical worldview.

"As an educator [Darryl], a lawyer [Joel], and an engineer [myself], we brought a wide variety of perspectives and experience to the table," said Ken Ekstrom. "We also came from three different denominational backgrounds. This diversity continued to be reflected in the initial board of directors, which included the three of us plus a pastor, an engineer, and two medical doctors with these four representing another three denominations."

Hurricane Mitch brought these people working for relief in Nicaragua to their knees praying together. When they stood up after Hurricane Mitch, they were still together in ways they had never imagined.

## Abelina Creates a New Life

Twelve years after the mudslide destroyed her village and killed so many of her family,

*The 1998 mudslide cut a V-shaped gash in La Casita, a gash still visible twelve years later, but slowly healing.*

Abelina sometimes tells her story to visitors at Casita Memorial Park, created atop the mudslide where El Porvenir's unrecovered dead are buried. Each tree in its sixty-acre tropical garden commemorates a person who is no more.

"That was a hard day," she said quietly to one visiting group. She choked up, paused. Then she continued with the impassive dignity of a woman who has weathered great pain.

In Santa Maria, she has become a community leader, she said. She grows *maize* (corn) and papayas in her garden and sells them. Others in the community sell handcrafted items aided by the Food for the Hungry's Nicamade program. When Abelina talks about her garden and her community work, her impassive mask evaporates. She is radiant with hope. She is a woman made new.

*El Limonal home*

# 04

# Walking in the Triangle of Death

*The place where God calls you is the place where your deep gladness and the world's deep hunger meet.*

-FREDERICK BUECHNER, WRITER AND THEOLOGIAN

Nicaraguans have a special name for the place where the small village of El Limonal sits north-west of Managua. They call it the Triangle of Death, because the village sits on a triangle of land surrounded by a dump, a sewer system, and a cemetery. This is home to some one thousand people.

Here is where some of the Nicaraguans whose villages had been destroyed by Hurricane Mitch have resettled. The villagers make their living scavenging the city dump; the pall and acrid smell of its smoke fill the air.

Electric wires—scavenged from the dump, with bare wire showing in spots—hang in a tangled crisscross a mere six or seven feet from the ground. The makeshift electric grid taps illegally into the wires passing the edge of town. Women do laundry outdoors on scrub boards, then hang it to dry on lines strung across their yards.

There is a school in this village—right next to a penitentiary. The area joke is that El Limonal residents go directly from one institution to the other.

Occasionally cars pass through the

*El Limonal dump*

AT A GLANCE
*Electricity*

About half of the electric power in Nicaragua is legally obtained. The other half is illegally siphoned—which is a major reason why electric lines are often strung helter-skelter. Only about half of the bills for legal electricity are paid—contributing to a high cost for electricity in the country. The Nehemiah Center does not have hot water because of the cost of electricity.

narrow dirt streets, passengers invisible behind tinted glass, tossing clothing from car windows, some of it winter wools from North America— useless in a country where the temperature rarely drops below seventy degrees. The cars travel on without stopping, while villagers rush from their homes to check for the occasional usable t-shirt or pair of sandals. Sometimes they find clothing with fabric that can be salvaged to stitch together curtains or chair covers. The remainder clutters the streets until someone carts it to the dump for burning.

North Americans looking for an example of a place in need of transformation certainly could point to this place, the so-called Triangle of Death.

## Transformation: Radical and Complex

What does the Nehemiah Center mean by the word "transformation"? Nehemiah Center leaders are seeking two-way transformations, which is a radical concept.

They aren't just seeking to transform the lives of Nicaraguans. The Nehemiah Center seeks to transform itself—itself as an institution—as well as the lives of all who touch that institution whether they are long-term or short-term visitors, Nicaraguans, South Americans, North Americans, or from somewhere else. And, it seeks to turn those people whom it has touched into agents of transformation themselves.

This is reflected in the organization's mission—"To develop integral agents of transformation who are grounded in a Christ-centered, biblical worldview . . ." The Nehemiah Center seeks mutual learning and collaboration not only locally but also internationally to transform communities and nations.

As defined by Joel Huyser, one of the Nehemiah Center's founders, transformation is an integral, ongoing, God-initiated process through which our broken relationships with God, self, neighbor, and creation are being restored.

It is a difficult concept: by its very nature it is a moving target. It is a goal to strive for, but never actually obtained. It ever evolves. Transformation is conversion—a continual conversion.

"We often think of conversion as the moment at which a person accepts Jesus as his or her personal savior. And, certainly, that is an important and defining moment of conversion," said

Joel. "Yet, those of us who have walked with Jesus for a while also know that the Christian life is one of a constant call to conversion. The Christian life is dynamic, not static. If we are growing into Jesus, we will daily be presented with fresh opportunities to take up our cross and follow him. Sometimes these will require a dramatic about-face on our part—so much so that we might even call it a second conversion."

Said Kim Freidah Brown, formerly with Food for the Hungry: "We're looking for end-to-end transformation for the whole chain of partners in ministry. The person in Canada who writes a check and the person in a Nicaraguan village who gets training or disaster relief, providers of funding, trainers, trainees, short- and long-term volunteers, paid staff, Nicaraguans, North Americans—the whole chain is being transformed."

Transforming monetary donors and the recipients is perhaps the most obvious example of transformation. At a workshop, Kim learned more about it: "Donors are not holy ATM machines. And they are not on a higher level, handing things down out of pity. Giving is a privilege, and everyone has something to give. Mutual giving and lasting transformation rise out of relationships."

As she spoke, Kim paused, pushing her hair back from her face, sweat beading on her forehead from the Nicaraguan heat. "Of course, we have not yet arrived."

*El Limonal mother and children*

*El Limonal child at play*

## Mike and Maria Saeli

*Mike and Maria Saeli*

Getting to El Limonal was a long journey from upstate New York, where Mike and Maria Saeli lived. Mike was an organic farmer and Maria a registered nurse. The Saelis met in college, married in 1972, and within a year were off to Micronesia (islands east of the Philippines) to follow Mike's longtime dream of being a Peace Corps volunteer.

After two years spent among a very communal group of people in Micronesia, the couple and their new baby moved to upstate New York, where Mike joined the family farm business. That is where they lived and raised their family for twenty-five years.

Nagging in the back of their minds during these years was a sense that they were called to work in missions. Mike took a mission trip to Mexico in 1996; Maria went to Germany in 1998. They both went to Brazil in 2000 and again in 2002. Though Maria heard God's call, Mike wasn't convinced.

Not until that 2002 trip to Brazil.

Mike's job on that short-term trip was to make cement blocks with a tiny block-making machine. The program director had set up two breaks each day for the volunteers to interact with neighborhood school children. The first day Mike kept working without the breaks.

He remembered, "On the second day, the Holy Spirit said to me, 'If you think all you came here to do is make blocks, you could have stayed home and done that. Stop and get to know these kids.'"

Mike stopped. He met Amanda. "Over the next four days . . . " Mike paused a full thirty seconds holding back tears. "I was ambushed by God's emissary, Amanda. God used Amanda to show me what my calling was. My reason for being there shifted from making blocks to listening to this girl and hearing her dreams and realizing how little chance she had without the mission school she was going to.

"When we left, I cried like a baby, and she was the one who comforted me. She said to me, 'It is going to be okay.' And she was right."

Within a short time, Mike and Maria were on their way to the *departamento* (province) of

León in Nicaragua with Mercy Ships, an organization that chiefly operates hospital ships to help people in developing countries. Initially, the Saelis and Mercy Ships became heavily involved in providing relief after Hurricane Mitch. However, by the end of 2004, the organization opted to close its operation in Nicaragua to focus elsewhere. Having fallen in love with the area, the Saelis chose to stay.

They continued their work in Nicaragua as part of Food for the Hungry, one of the Nehemiah Center's international partners.

Becoming part of the Nehemiah Center umbrella was itself transformational for the Saelis. They were attracted to the center's collaboration of different organizations and different denominations, working together to bring cultural change in multiple arenas: agriculture, health, Christian education, microenterprise, arts, media, and more.

"This was a multifaceted, holistic ministry that reflected kingdom values outside and within the organizations, and we had never seen that before," said Mike. "It really began to open my eyes to how the kingdom of God is meant to work that I had never seen before.

"With Mercy Ships, we understood that it was about more than the spiritual message but also hope and healing—the two hands of the gospel," Mike said. "But this was even bigger. It blew the sides out of the box for what composed ministry in a holistic way. We began to be introduced to a biblical worldview. We began to read Darrow Miller [and others] and began to understand a

broader philosophy of what comprises Christian development work in a developing nation. That lit something inside of me and something inside of Maria."

That transformation was just one part of their continuing transformation.

Mike said, "Although you really can't divide it, part of my soul-side transformation happened in Nicaragua. I didn't look at my watch. People don't even own one! Nicaragua is event-oriented. You come to a meeting because your friends are there and you want to spend time with them. Yes, there is something to be accomplished, but that is not the emphasis.

"I have also come to appreciate the hugging, touching, and warmth of Nicaraguan culture. We found change happening not through programs or technology, but through relationships . . . It was and is a fantastic learning curve to be here."

Beginning in August 2006, Mike and Maria

*Maria Saeli and a young El Limonal friend*

FROM CAROL'S JOURNAL
## *Different Eyes*

When I ride the streets of Nicaragua's capital city, Managua, I see block after block of poverty.

Then I visit El Limonal.

It is two hundred huts filled with residents who eke out an existence rescuing bottles, cans, and cardboard from the dump.

I assess it, walking the dirt streets with Maria Saeli of Food for the Hungry, and find a new category: extreme poverty.

*Doing laundry*

Maria hugs three children selling from a food stand. She admires a puppy one woman is grooming. She asks a woman hand-laundering clothes how many days' work are on the line behind her.

'*Tres dias* (three days),' is the shy answer.

She says El Limonal now has electricity and water. She stops to ask a man what plants he is watering in his new garden.

Where I see poverty, Maria sees progress.

While I despair, Maria hopes. She also fosters hope.

Lord, give me Maria's eyes. For they are your eyes, too, I think. And let my hands, like hers, be yours as well.

Saeli started walking alongside the people of El Limonal. Although newly-arrived North Americans are blown away by the poverty and need, Mike and Maria see progress—progress in nutrition and health, progress in education, and progress in microbusinesses.

One hot summer day, Maria took two North American short-term volunteers on a tour of the village. As they walked the dirt streets, she pointed to progress and beauty. She stopped to admire a dog, hugged children selling from a roadside stand and gently reminded one of them to put his candy wrapper away. "*Basura aqui* (garbage goes here)," she said, pointing to a trash can. As the trio walked under a jerry-rigged tangle of wires, Maria's umbrella pole touched one of the wires. When the North Americans agitatedly told her, she calmly lowered it and kept on walking.

Making use of Nehemiah Center training programs, the Saelis and others have started promoting family gardens—on the villagers' patios, which are big enough for one-meter-by-three-meter gardens.

The successes:

Fátima Medina is a natural community leader and has been trained as an agent of transformation. Her garden was the first pilot project. Now, she works with others to help them establish their own gardens. When the women scavenge the dump, she teaches them how to collect organic material to use for compost on their gardens. She is teaching the El Limonal women to garden organically in ways that benefit their families.

Estela Maldonado had never planted a

seed in her life. Now, she marvels at seeing things grow and experiments with them. She asked people for their squash seeds and also saved them from plants that had done well and planted them. She grows both peppers and squash from seed. She plants and grows with confidence, supplementing family nutritional needs—and she has new self-esteem. She has mastered a new skill. "It was important for her to believe in herself—she was made in the image of God," said Maria.

Four women from the village started making jewelry and doubled their family income. They were doing so well, they decided to add a fifth woman to their group. Empowered to make something beautiful with their hands, they also decided to help someone else.

Yet, for all the successes, they are outnumbered by the opportunities:

As she walked, Maria broke a twig from a Moringa tree alongside the road. Called the friend of pregnant women, the tree leaves brim with nutrition. She ticked off the nutrition in just three tablespoons of dry powder made from these leaves: Four times the calcium of milk, seven times the

---

### FROM CAROL'S JOURNAL
## *On Garbage and Garments*

En route from the airport to our guest house, warm wind against my face through the taxi window, I watch Managua pass. The street sides are peppered with miscellaneous bottles, cans, plastic bags, newspaper, and cardboard. "Disgusting," I think. Miss Reinders' fifth grade anti-littering lessons are still burned into my brain. "Surely, they could do *something* about this mess!"

Through the same window, I see women with matched jewelry and perfectly groomed hair, men in crisp white shirts, and children in immaculate navy-and-white school uniforms. I remember the words from the Nehemiah Center team training guide: "Please wear modest and neat clothing. Americans have a reputation for being the sloppiest people on the streets."

At Sunday worship, my all-cotton wraparound is perfectly pressed, no thanks to me. When I asked Judy, the thirteen-year-old daughter of our guesthouse hosts, if I could use an ironing board, she said, "Let me press it for you." It is that wraparound's very first outing without a single wrinkle.

When I ask about this Nicaraguan double standard, Joel Huyser tells me a Nicaraguan proverb: *Lavaste la cara, el mono no* (One washes one's face, but not one's derriere). Its point, he tells me, is that it is important to be neat and clean in public—to have a clean "face."

And the streets? Well, they are like the derriere; they don't need to be clean. He points out that different subcultures, for who knows what reason, develop different fixations for order and cleanliness. For some, it's a manicured front lawn, for others a spotless car riding to Sunday morning worship.

Heading back to the airport, a month later, I haven't lost my distaste for litter. But then, I haven't mastered the art of a perfect press, either.

vitamin C of oranges, four times the vitamin A of carrots, three times the potassium of bananas, two times the protein of yogurt—and many other vitamins. "It produces leaves year round and grows rapidly," she said with excitement. Then her voice grew wistful. "I wish all the women would use it. It would make so much difference. But some are starting."

The smoke-filled air and poor sanitation system continue to cause ongoing health issues. Lung disease and diarrhea are commonplace in the village. Fifteen to twenty women from the village have completed a Community Health Evangelism (CHE) health course offered through the Nehemiah Center to understand these issues. "They have begun to share it with others," said Maria. "They are beginning to see that it is worth the risk: 'My neighborhood—my neighbor's lack of a latrine, the smoke from the dump—affect me.' They know that for their health, their whole community needs to change."

The Saelis acknowledge that progress is slow—and sometimes they even see regression. Change frequently is short-lived. But they are encouraged, Mike said, by the words often attributed to Archbishop Oscar Romero, who was assassinated in 1980 while saying mass in San Salvador. Seated in their tiny apartment in the city of León, Mike pulled a book from the shelf above his computer workstation and read it: "We accomplish in our lifetime only a tiny fraction of the magnificent enterprise that is God's work. Nothing we do is complete, which is a way of saying that the kingdom always lies beyond us."

# David and Wendy Van Klinken

*David and Wendy Van Klinken*

Three to four hours northeast of Managua is the Mount Mombachito region. The crater side of this extinct volcano is a rural area with fertile volcanic soil and the place a half-dozen Mombachito coffee farmers and their families call home.

The farmers, part of the Mombachito land bank, bought their three-acre plots with loans provided by the Farmer-to-Farmer program of Partners Worldwide. Here, they grow coffee beans to sell and food for their families. The story of these people is transformational on many levels, starting with their North American partners, the Van Klinkens.

For several years up until the start of 2011, the Van Klinkens worked as liaisons between the

North American organization, Partners Worldwide, and the farmers of Nicaragua. They served as liaisons for eighty-five farm families in three areas of Nicaragua: Matagalpa, Boaco, and Mombachito.

Long before they ever heard of Mombachito, David and Wendy Van Klinken lived a rich life in their home in Sunnyside, Washington, where David was a farm manager for the owner of a large farming conglomerate and Wendy a nurse for a clinic. They were lifelong members of the Sunnyside Christian Reformed Church, and lived very comfortable lives.

For one memorable vacation, the Van Klinkens drove well over a thousand miles in their new SUV to San Diego, staying at $250 four-star bed-and-breakfasts each night en route. They flew their three children—then ages sixteen, fifteen, and ten—to the Los Angeles airport, and spent five days showing them the sites—Disneyland, Knott's Berry Farm, Six Flags Magic Mountain, and others—before sending them home on a return flight. The couple then continued their SUV travel, breakfasting one morning alongside Mel Torme's wife and daughter while overlooking a California bay at La Jolla.

"With two high-paying jobs, we lived a wealthy family lifestyle, almost beyond our means. We thought nothing of going to dinner with several friends and spending a thousand dollars," said Wendy. "Our lives were not exemplary."

In 1997, following Wendy's fortieth birthday party, the Van Klinkens received what they describe as a bonk on the head. After the party, David had left home in the middle of the night to travel to a distant farm. On his return trip, a half-mile from home his pager went off at 7 a.m.—his home number. His daughter greeted him with, "Dad, I can't wake Mom up."

"She was gray, had no pulse, and wasn't breathing," David remembered. "I started CPR and told our daughter to call 911. After five minutes she started to respond."

At the emergency room, physicians told him that Wendy would live, but she would never be the same. She had been without oxygen for too long.

David prayed, "Lord, I know you can move mountains. All I want is my wife back."

At 5 p.m. that afternoon, Wendy was back in her own bed, in her words, "feeling run over by a truck, but everything was clear."

What had happened to Wendy at the restaurant party? David and Wendy say they will never know the physical details for sure. She exhibited all the symptoms of eating a toxic food or having a drug such as Ecstasy slipped into her drink. They do know it was surely a turning point, a catalyst God provided to tell them they could be of use to him.

Short-term mission trips began to tug at them, and they eventually said yes. In 2000, David volunteered in Zambia, Africa; Wendy traveled to Nicaragua for disaster relief at the same time. In 2002, they both made a trip to the Nehemiah Center.

Then in February 2003 while in Afghanistan working in agriculture, David had what he calls a "life-changing" moment. Scheduled to be there for just ten days, he and a couple companions drove five hours on a dirt road to catch their return flight, but there were no airplanes at the Kabul airport. They were told to return in a week or two. They made the five-hour trek back to Jalalabad, and waited sans phone, sans computer, sans any contact with home. On the second trip to the Kabul airport, they were delayed by three flat tires. "I was very concerned we would miss our flight again as we had yet another very low tire one mile from the airport," David said.

Held up in traffic, David looked at the bombed-out wreckage of Kabul. He saw three young boys barefoot in the snow trying to stay warm by a fire. "One looked like my grandson. I told God, 'Okay, that's it. I don't know what it is you will have me do, but I am going to do something. I will be your hands because I don't want that to be a life my grandson has to live.'"

Ultimately, God led them to Nicaragua—which they knew would be a contrast to their Washington lifestyle. "Our moving was a shock to all because we had lived in the same house for twenty-seven years, had solid jobs, were never without work, had a strong Dutch work ethic. It blew them out of the water," said Wendy. "Three hundred people's jaws dropped in church when we announced our plans. Some said 'You are crazy. What are you thinking?'"

That thought probably crossed the couple's minds as well—especially in the first few months in their new country.

Learning Spanish was tougher than they had expected. David caught dengue fever. They missed home, family, and friends, and didn't have a place to live. They didn't know Nicaraguan culture—where to go to the bank or the grocery store—until a missionary couple took them under their wing.

Two weeks after the Van Klinken's arrival, a friend asked David via cell phone how he was doing. David responded, "Aside from the fact that a month ago I was sitting in a four-star restaurant and now we are living in a room in someone else's house, and smoke fills it every morning when tortillas are cooked, and the shower is cold water—all things considered, we are doing okay."

Looking back, David said, "There had been a very big transformation of lifestyle."

Those four-star hotels were replaced by nights at a Boaco hotel with service-and-learning teams—a tank of brown water and a dipping bowl for a shower, a bucket of water poured as needed for a flush. A vacation getaway became a trip to a $33-per-night musty cabin with monkeys howling in the adjacent forest, a nearby lake filled with fish and ducks, and walks through cool and pristine mountains.

In Nicaragua, the couple lived in a modest two-bedroom apartment, a fraction of the size of the U.S. home they sold, with a kitchen "just big enough for one person to turn around in," Wendy said. The apartment's one luxury was a Lazy-boy recliner.

And yet, when the daughter of their translator Rolando Mejía spent a day and night with them, she reported to her father, "I felt like a princess. There was a queen-sized bed—and no holes in the ceiling. It was so different. I had to sleep with the lights on."

## The Coffee Farmers of Mount Mombachito

Submitted photo

*Gary Baker (left) and Freddy Guadamuz pour coffee beans into a depulping machine while Gary's grand-son Josh Mulder looks on.*

Of the six families who are part of the Mombachito land bank, almost all were once day laborers, working on coffee plantations owned by others, with little hope of ever owning land. Those coffee plantations only provide seasonal work for the day laborers. The extremely low wages force entire families, including children who should be in school, to work during the harvesting season. Unfortunately, the children of these day laborers face a similar life. The grinding poverty is inherited from one generation to the next.

Through land banks, Partners Worldwide provides loans that give families the first opportunity they have ever had to own land. As the families repay their loans, the money goes into a revolving fund that will help more farmers purchase land.

Ricardo Rodríguez is the natural leader of the group of Mombachito farmers. He paid off his loan and now owns his farm outright. Most of the farmers will pay off their loans in seven years; a few might take eight years. These farmers work hard, harvesting the beans between November and January, handpicking the beans based on their color.

They are largely self-sufficient—something that David and Wendy insisted on. "An important question for us to ask ourselves—if we walked away today, could they manage?" said David. "Could they carry on?"[1]

When, for example, the Mombachito farmers decided they wanted goats, they asked for a loan. Wendy and David told them it was a good idea. A month later, the farmers had the same request: We want goats. Wendy and David again told them they thought it was a good idea. But it wasn't until the farmers actually built a fence and goat house that the project got moving. The farmers first had to pay out of their own pockets for a structure, a water source, and plants to feed the goats. Only then were they ready for a loan to purchase the goats.

[1]Wendy and David Van Klinken started transitioning back to the United States in February 2010 when their daughter was diagnosed with cancer. Wendy moved to support their daughter, and David followed by February 2011. Their daughter is now cancer-free, and the Van Klinkens are back home in Washington state. Freddy Guadamuz, a native of Managua, serves now as the liaison for seventy-nine farmers (a part-time job) and Rolando Mejía, a full-time pastor, serves as the liaison for the six Mombachito coffee farmers. Both Freddy and Rolando have served as translators for the teams and know the program well. David Van Klinken expects the transition to be a smooth one.

## Text from a Bag of Mombachito Coffee Beans

˙In November 2004, eight coffee farmers began a journey to fulfill their dream. With a loan from Partners Worldwide in Grand Rapids, Michigan, these eight farmers purchased a small coffee plantation near the 3,000 foot level in the partial sun shadows of Mt. Mombachito North East of Boaco, Nicaragua.

˙From the inception the Mombachito coffee farmers agreed their finished product would be limited to the highest quality possible. Beginning with the proper balance of shade and sun, Mombachito coffee plants are organically hand maintained prior to a labor filled hand select harvest, finishing with a meticulous sorting to assure only the finest beans proceed to the roasting process.

˙The blending of attention to detail and the natural aroma of the high tropic microclimate of Mt. Mombachito unite to capture the essence of this fine Nicaraguan coffee.

˙Thank you much for purchasing the fruit of the labors of the Mombachito Coffee Growers.˙

Submitted photo

*Brevon Jasper and Melvin Rodríguez carry Mombachito coffee beans from the field.*

It was an important lesson for the Mombachito farmers to learn. Previous government programs that have given out pigs, chickens, and cows failed when Nicaraguans didn't have anything to feed the animals. Instead of raising the animals, they ate them. In contrast, the Mombachito farmers were prepared for the responsibility and have their goats. The terms of the loan: When the nannies have babies they need to pass on the babies to other farmers whom they themselves have trained to raise goats. That is their repayment.

When it came to the processing of the Mombachito coffee beans, David and Wendy took a similar approach. They bought a hundred pounds of green coffee, roasted and packaged it, created a label, and showed the farmers the package. The farmers observed and saw how they themselves were making $1.40 per pound for coffee that later sold for $5 per pound. They took over much of the processing themselves. In 2009, they exported 1,500 bags of coffee to Iowa. In 2011, the farmers started marketing it themselves and began finding their own markets in Nicaragua.

## The Farmers Talk

Francisco, a single twenty-four-year-old, became one of the coffee farmers when he was twenty. "I am the first in my family to own land. They feel happy because I have this chance to own my own parcel. My father and brothers give me a hand. My sister, too," said Francisco.

"Since the first day I have started working on this farm, I have my dream. I never imagined myself to have a chance to have my own land and to work for myself." Francisco wrote a testimonial about his transformation:

Submitted photo

*Francisco Gonzales*

Hello, I am Francisco Javier Gonzalez. I live at the village called Mombachito. I used to be a farm worker, who worked for other farmers as I had to support my family. One day, I was hired as a worker [day laborer] for other Mombachito land bank farmers.

Thus, I was working for them for six months. I never imagined that they were only testing me at work habits. One day two beneficiaries [farmers] from the land bank and brother Gersan decided to have a meeting, and they invited me to this meeting.

Then, they proposed me to become the owner of one of the parcels. I now understood that they were testing me [before]. At that moment, I could not believe it! I had such great opportunity to become one of the owners and to manage my own land.

[When they invited me to be a farmer in Mombachito,] I believed that it was only a dream, but brothers Ricardo and Carlos told me that it was not only a dream—it was true. Since that time, I felt that my life will be changed forever.

It was a great joy to me that I would take part and become one of the owners of the land bank. At that time, I went back to my parents' home and told them about such great news. They were very happy, but still they did not believe it.

I was so excited that I came back to the farm (Mombachito) and asked them again! They were laughing when they told me that it was true. They confirmed it by showing me the minutes of the meeting, which the three of them have signed.

They approved the fact that I had passed the test as a good worker. Then, I signed the contract, and since then I work on my own farm. I farm with much affection, and therefore I call it *La Primavera* (the Springtime) Farm.

Now I give my thanks to God, our brothers and sisters from the Farmer-to-Farmer program, and Partners Worldwide for giving me this great opportunity. I now am trained to work on this small parcel, in which we can grow our foods to support my family easier.

I give my thanks to God one more time, and for Wendy and David, who have trained us to become small exporters for the Mombachito organic coffee. Therefore, I have been able to make the repayments for my parcel.

I am a young man filled with much joy and lots of dreams and hope to move forward. I hope in God that you will continue visiting us since you have become a great support to us.

*Francisco Javier Gonzalez*

## Passing It On

*Wendy Van Klinken snuggles a Mombachito baby.*

The pride, hope, and self-esteem of these farmers make this story a success, a transformational success. As inspirational as this is, their story gets better.

Down the road from the Mombachito farmers is a prison that houses twenty-five to forty military prisoners for three months to two years. One day while visiting their interpreter's Bible study at the prison, the Van Klinkens learned the prisoners had little to eat and little to do, but the prison did have some unused land available.

When prison administrators asked for help in starting a garden, the Van Klinkens suggested it to the Mombachito farmers, and then waited.

A couple months later, as the Van Klinkens were visiting the farmers, Maria Luisa had a message for Rolando, the Van Klinken's interpreter: "We would like to go to the prison."

The Mombachito farmers offered to provide starter plants, soil, and compost from their supplies. Rolando offered to find tires to shield the starter gardens from the grubs. David agreed to provide the transportation to haul the supplies to the prison.

"This is huge," said Wendy. "It is working. They are transformed and passing on their transformation to others. They are passing it on."

That is what the Nehemiah Center means by transformation: Those who are transformed become agents of transformation.

Admittedly, the Van Klinkens weren't always willing to step back and let the farmers learn to make their own decisions and take responsibility. At first, David said, he approached his work in the same way he managed a 20,000-acre farm in the United States. He thought the buck stopped with him. He had to make a decision quickly and correctly—and then he had to get others to go along with it.

Wendy had the same mentality. As a nurse she saw a problem, diagnosed it, fixed it with meds, and moved on. In time, however, she learned that no cream would permanently get rid of the scabies from a baby who continued to play with animals. Nor would insulin help a diabetic without any refrigeration. "We needed to teach different eating habits; we needed to provide health education in prevention," said Wendy.

David learned to walk alongside the farmers. "It works much better to walk the farmer's land, find out how his family is, how he is doing, and keep at it long enough until I find something that really impresses me. Then I say, 'I'm impressed by that. Can you teach me how to do it?' That opens the door for suggestions that I may make."

As David and Wendy Van Klinken walked with the farmers in their small fields, so Mike and Maria Saeli walk with the residents in the Triangle of Death. These two couples first needed transformation in their own lives before they could begin to walk alongside others in their own personal journeys toward transformation.

The real beauty of these stories is the multiplication power. Economic leaders often boast of the multiplication effect when describing how a new event or new business helps many businesses, which in turn creates business for other companies. The Van Klinkens and the Saelis are examples of a more far-reaching multiplication blessing. Their lives demonstrate how the transformation of individuals can lead to the transformation of a country.

*Nehemiah Center guest house*

# 05

## Piercing Hearts

*I heard someone from a team say this week, "Time is money. Come on. Come on. Let's go." It sounded so strange to me because time is not money here. It took me a while to realize that North America is different but not necessarily better. And, Nicaragua is not necessarily better. A good place is probably somewhere in between.*

*- DAVE BOONE, A MODESTO, CALIFORNIA, NATIVE WORKING*

*THROUGH MISSIONARY VENTURES IN NICARAGUA*

The relationships and the transformations that have taken place in the hearts of the El Limonal villagers, the Saelis, the Van Klinkens, and the Mombachito coffee farmers have taken place over years. These are people who have made long-term commitments.

That is just one part of the equation. The Nehemiah Center also seeks transformation in the lives of people who make shorter visits to Nicaragua. As it explains in its training manual for newcomers:

"The Nehemiah Center facilitates interchanges of cultural experiences of service and learning between Nicaraguan and North American Christians in that all participants deepen their understanding and commitment to a biblical worldview and strengthen their capacity to cause positive impacts in their lives, churches, and communities."

What the center is striving for is not your average short-term mission trip.

Google "short-term missions" and you'll find thousands of opportunities available. You'll find sites that offer opportunities to college students, to teenagers, to adults, to church groups. You'll find sites that tell you "things to know before you go," sites that offer insurance, sites that offer training to organize such trips. One site (christianvolunteering.org) boasts over five thousand short-term mission and volunteer opportunities.

Between one million and four million North American Christians reportedly participated in short-term mission trips in 2003.[1] If you haven't gone on one, then, if you are a North American who attends church even occasionally, you have probably sat through a talk given by someone who has been on one. "Culture shock," you heard them say, "such poverty." "We built a school, a latrine, a house, a church." "It makes me appreciate what we have."

For some North Americans, that is what a short-term mission trip is:  a brief eye-opening experience. And those living in third-world countries probably don't see it much differently: a brief visit from Santa Claus.

There have been some who have questioned the value of these short-term mission trips—people like John Lee, a pastor at Bethel Christian Reformed Church in Sioux Center, Iowa. He was a CRC missionary in Nicaragua for four years before he went to the seminary.

> My personal experience with work teams was initially negative. While living in Belize during a semester at college, I saw a steady stream of teams pass through the local church I attended and the orphanage I volunteered at after services.  I was generally cynical, noting the logistical burdens, time away from ministry, and mild irritants placed on the local church in its new role as perpetual host.  I wondered about the long-term effects on orphan children of transient caregivers.  I watched kids go through punctuated periods of bonding and pampering only to be "abandoned" once again.  I also generally saw work teams as inefficient vehicles for service. I especially remember one afternoon in Belmopan watching several North American teenagers mowing a lawn in front of the church.  I remember thinking, "In a land of high unemployment, do we really need such expensive, unskilled labor?"  And what does that imply to the national church?  Does it strip them of dignity?  Of initiative? Of communal responsibility?[2]

Kurt Ver Beek, a professor of sociology and third-world development at Calvin College in Grand Rapids, Michigan, is even more cynical. He surveyed 127 North Americans who helped build homes for Hondurans after Hurricane Mitch. He also spoke to seventy-eight Hondurans and concluded neither group experienced notable life changes.  He also concluded that monetary donations to missions by short-timers—an argument often used to justify short-term trips—only increases marginally.

> While I was surprised about the lack of impact of short-term missions, I don't think I should have been. I'm beginning to see that short-term missions are like the rest of life. We get to a conference or a summer camp and leave excited to pray every

---

[1] Abram Huyser Honig, "Study questions whether short-term missions make a difference," *Christianity Today,* <www.christianitytoday.com/ct/article_print.html?id=34571> (December 1, 2010).

[2] "Short-Term Work Teams, Modern Keys to Kingdom Living," a paper by John Lee.

day, exercise four times a week, and reorganize our closets. But then we get home to find we are behind at work, the kids have soccer practice and we have to pay off the credit card. Our new-found motivation tapers off. Participants in short-term missions have similar experiences. Immediately after returning from a trip, participants *intend* to make changes in their life, but usually fall back into old routines.[3]

## The Nehemiah Center's Service and Learning Institute

The Nehemiah Center isn't immune to these challenges.  The questions raised by John Lee are good ones, and the situation that Kurt Ver Beek paints obviously happens.

The Service and Learning Institute is the Nehemiah Center's way of facilitating mission trips in ways that are helpful, not harmful. Trip lengths vary. Some are one-time, short-term mission trips. Some churches make regular short-term trips and have developed an ongoing relationship with Nicaraguans. Some trips are a little longer, perhaps a month or more. The Nehemiah Center *Steve Holtrop* also works with students serving internships in Nicaragua or who are in the country as part of a semester-long experience—developing cross-cultural learning and even mentoring opportunities. As director of the Nehemiah Center's Service and Learning Institute, Steve Holtrop focuses on how the two cultures can learn together, and on how all those involved can expand their understanding of who God is and how he wants us to be.

*Short-term logistics*

The international partners of the Nehemiah Center vary in the extent to which they handle their own logistics and programming as opposed to coordinating through the Service and Learning Institute.

The details vary tremendously, but most often, ten to fifteen people make up the short-term teams and stay about ten days.  From the start of 2004 through February 2011, the Nehemiah Center hosted 198 groups totaling 2,336 people—an average of about twenty-eight groups per year.[4]

Before undertaking a trip, teams receive a 32-page "Pre-field Information Guide" to read, think about, and study. Besides offering extensive background about Nicaragua and the Nehemiah Center itself, the guide also provides a myriad of details about the trip. It encourages visitors to

---

[3]"Are Short-Term Missions Good Stewardship?" *Christianity Today*, July 5, 2005, <www.christianitytoday.com/ct/article_print.html?id=34558> (December 1, 2010).

[4]Teams are coordinated by different organizations and come for different purposes. Coordinating organizations include Caribbean Ministries, Christian Reformed World Missions, Christian Reformed World Relief Committee, EduDeo, Food for the Hungry, Missionary Ventures International, and Worldwide Christian Schools (US and Canada). Although a dual purpose is present for all teams, some focus more on service, others more on learning.

FROM CAROL'S JOURNAL

## Transformation Past and Future

In April 2011, my church service-and-learning team tells our Pella, Iowa, congregation what we have seen and heard in Managua and Chinandega.

It was an intense week for us the previous February—watching, listening, and learning. We learned about youth leadership training and the Nehemiah Center's healthy church program. We walked with Nicaraguans to houses in a destitute neighborhood, praying with and for some of the residents. We attended a Wednesday evening outdoor service and were asked to lead two worship songs. We met students who had attended arts camps.

The theme of the DVD in which we now share our collected impressions with the congregation goes beyond "I learned how good we have it here." It has inklings of transformation. Our pastor, Gary Hanson, says he came back with the overwhelming question: "How much do I really need?"

Kathy Groenenboom, a grandmother who especially enjoyed the children of Chinandega, says she sensed a less-uptight quality in Nicaraguan life. "I laughed in Nicaragua more than I have in a long time."

Harley Janssen, a young engineer and father of four, says, "The type of community we had there felt right, but at the same time to get there [to this kind of community] requires you to not be defined by your possessions, by who you know, or by the jobs and goals you have. All of a sudden we've given up an awfully lot of what we cling to. And consequently we found community. That's scary!"

Ed Spoelstra says he saw a willingness to take risks. "We saw an after-school Compassion program with a hundred fifty kids. . . Here, we have to have our t's crossed and i's dotted, the coffee made, and the cookies ready [before we take action]," he said. "They [the Chinandega Compassion program founders] didn't do that. They started the program with sponsors for only three kids. We probably would have said it's not worth it."

And retiree Claude Zylstra prays for the church universal, in Nicaragua and North America, "that beautiful things will happen. That we may adopt the same principles. . ."

Our two-way transformation has begun. Our team has named our congregation's long-term relationship Friends of Chinandega, and—with church council approval—is moving ahead with a six-part program we drafted in the hot and humid lobby of Don Mario hotel in downtown Chinandega.

That plan includes ongoing communication with Nicaraguan companion churches, mutual prayer support, value-add projects for sales of Nicaraguan crafts, sponsorship of children through Compassion International, ongoing support of Nicaraguan arts camps, and launching arts camps for at-risk children in Pella.

It is an ambitious launch; we are not assured of success.

When we had doubts as we sweated out a plan in the hotel lobby, our pastor reminded us of the Nicaraguans we had seen. "We need to give ourselves the freedom to fail," he said.

The freedom to fail.

In the months to come, I want to keep walking the path of that new-found freedom.

learn as much as they can ahead of time about the country, its history, its language, and its people. Perhaps even more importantly, the guide discusses how visitors might benefit themselves from the trip.

The costs are significant. In 2011, participants were expected to pay $500 (U.S.) per person for a donation to the specific project they would be working on, in addition to $600 per person as a donation to the Nehemiah Center for its ministries and to cover the expenses for the trip (meals, lodging, transportation, etc.). Participants also are responsible for the costs for their own transportation to and from Nicaragua.

Frequently, groups meet among themselves prior to the trips. Veterans may share their experiences, and everyone shares their enthusiasm.

*Long-term impacts*

Perhaps what makes these trips to the Nehemiah Center different from many is that the center's focus is not on the short-term impact but on the long-term transformation. Visitors aren't welcomed because of their anticipated *labor* but because of their anticipated *education*. Education—transformation—is the chief goal. That's why these teams are not just service teams but are service-and-*learning* teams.

"Americans have the financial resources that can help the transformation happen, but when the financing is seen as the answer to all of our poverty, it is essentially misunderstanding God," said Steve. "Financing is not all. It is only part of it. When that financing is directed in appropriate manners to encourage the greater understanding of who God is and who we are, then it makes a lot of sense."

It's common to hear comments from short-term visitors like "It was awesome," and "I have changed my thoughts on different things," and "I am going to do something." However, Steve admits that the Nehemiah Center doesn't have the resources to follow up on the service-and-learning teams to see what changes have been wrought; the attempts it has made have been inconclusive. After all, quantifying a change in heart is difficult.

Still, he is hopeful:

- One team included a father and a son who started the trip not talking to each other. The son, about eighteen years old, resented being forced to go. By the end of the trip, they were talking and relating as you would expect a father and son to do.
- A manager in a light fixture plant said he had never considered how his manager job should be done in a Christian manner. He vowed to change when he returned.
- A North American church group observed a Nicaraguan church working with prostitutes. It made the church reevaluate itself and begin a mission working with drug addicts in its own community.

More emphasis has been put recently on developing long-term relationships between

## 'I Knew I Would Be Going Back'

'My first trip to Nicaragua was overwhelming in the sense that I came home with a confused passion,' said Anna Van Rooselaar, a member of a Canadian service team who has made three trips to the Nehemiah Center. 'How could I leave a piece of my heart in Nicaragua after only ten days, and what was I going to do about it? I, who already have so much, received so much. I thought I was going there to give but ended up receiving so much kindness, hospitality, acceptance, insight into a different kind of poverty (lack of connectedness, community, relational-living, spiritual wholeness) and so much more. I came home feeling like I owed Nicaragua, a place and people now dear to my heart, so much because of all that I had been given, and I knew I would be going back.'

*Lourdes Rivas (standing in background) hosts dinner in her home for a Burlington, Ontario, church team.*

churches in North America and clusters of churches in Nicaragua. They both learn from each other and both learn what it means to take biblical worldview into their communities. Chapter 10 covers these partnerships in more detail.

Despite his early skepticism about the value of short-term mission trips, Pastor John Lee changed his mind about their value after working with more than thirty teams at the Nehemiah Center.

"Yes, teams can be extremely expensive . . . and yes, work team ministry can be conceived and executed poorly," he said. However, he added, "I've grown to appreciate the work that God is doing through short-term mission teams."

Long-term missionaries need to help guide the short-term trips, and education needs to be an integral part. "But perhaps the biggest impact of such ministry is the mutually beneficial synergy they foster," John added. "When done in the servant spirit of Christ, short-term team ministry provides a visible example of Christian unity to impressionable onlookers and a tremendous opportunity for both nationals and team members to gain a sharpened awareness of the Kingdom of God."

As part of that experience, too, John has found multiple examples of short-term mission trippers being stretched so far out of their comfort zone in a foreign country that they are then prone to stretch their comfort zone at home as well to reach out to marginalized people.

Changing hearts so that people are able

Submitted photo

*John Lee provides a ride for a young Nicaraguan.*

## 'This Is What Transformation Looks Like'

Transformation sometimes happens in unpredictable ways, evident in this story from John Lee.

'I was taking a work team to Chinandega, and I had to find them a place to stay. A pastor showed me a hotel. It looked okay, so we booked it. Then, when we arrived, I noticed the condom dispensers and slots in the doors [for making payments without being seen]. I saw the curtains for the carports [used to conceal vehicles] and I realized: I've got a work team staying in an auto hotel! I asked the pastor, and he said, yes, it had been an auto hotel [a hotel that rents hourly for trysts], but the owners had come to know Christ and they were changing it. And I thought, 'That is what transformation looks like—an auto hotel whose first other use is by a Christian work team.''

to change their lives when they return home is a goal of the Service and Learning Institute. It is essential that the transformation be two-directional, said Steve. "The North American Christian community needs to look at these missions. They need to say, 'We are spending a lot of money. What are we getting out of it?' If it is not bringing about transformation in both countries, then is it worth it?

"I don't want to say, though, 'how much is the learning worth?' But the investment is less wise if there is no transference. If their lives never change, then it might not be worth it."

As a team coordinator for Food for the Hungry (FH) in connection with the Nehemiah Center until mid-2009, Andrea Kamouyerou worked directly with a half-dozen short-term teams each year.

"I love the way we do teams here—the two-way learning. Both sides are learning from one another. We are all children of God and are in the process of God transforming us. We are walking alongside others also in the process in a different context. The Nicaraguan Christian has a lot to offer and vice versa. It's not project-based but relationship-based."

## Transformations on the North Side

Submitted photo

*Barb and Al Kopaska*

It was almost a fluke that Iowan Al Kopaska even noticed the blurb in a bulletin in 2000 about an upcoming mission trip for men to Nicaragua. Not a reader, he is now convinced it was divine intervention. Not only was it out of character for him to read the notice; it was also out of character for him to agree to make the trip. "I had never been that far from home in my life," he said.

Afterwards, when he returned to his home in Kellogg, Iowa, he was convinced that he wanted to go back to Nicaragua again with his wife, Barb, and he wanted to make changes in his life. An electrical contractor who also owned a hardware business in Kellogg, he decided he wanted to sell the business, sell his home, and build a smaller home in the nearby town of Pella.  He imagined a life where he and his wife could serve a couple months of every year in Nicaragua.

Al knows now that though his motives were good, he was still planning, still in control. He hadn't yet learned to follow God's lead.

After significant business losses coupled with the near-impossibility of selling the store and a recurring infection in his leg, Al finally got the message that he thinks God was sending him: Trust; don't plan.

"We bit off a huge chunk when we bought that business," said Al. "I knew I had a goal, and I had to meet it. I bought a backhoe, and I knew how many dollars that machine had to turn each month. It was a lot of pressure. I knew how many dollars it took for the store to have a good month. Keep pushing, you have to do more.

"But that is not where it is at."

Several times Al has returned to Nicaragua with Barb, but his dream that they might make regular and longer-term trips hasn't happened for them. Still, the impact of his experiences has been significant. Experiencing for himself life in Nicaragua while simultaneously experiencing so many downturns in his life in Iowa was a humbling experience. "The Lord took me to my knees, and he humbled me beyond anything you can imagine."

For Barb, too, the trips to Nicaragua affected the way she views her life. "You see them content with nothing. We come back and we have everything. We [as Americans] always find someone who has more than we do, and we don't feel like millionaires. But the earthly possessions aren't important anymore . . . We really tried to pull ourselves out of that and become servants, and be thankful and give.

"I have also learned a lot from Joel [Huyser] about worldview," Barb added. "Everything you do is accountable to God—the way you conduct your personal life, your financial life, your marriage."

Ultimately, Al and Barb did sell their store and move to Pella. And together they made four other trips to Nicaragua where Al often worked on construction projects. Barb, a school nurse, spent her time teaching CPR and first aid, sometimes in schools, sometimes in remote areas where people are hungry for the knowledge Barb can share.

For the time being, Al and Barb remain in Pella. Al continues to make calls for his electrical contracting business, simultaneously using those opportunities to sell bags of coffee from the Mombachito coffee farmers. "You got seven minutes?" he'll ask his clients, ready to whip out the short video about the farmers from his truck. Person-to-person, he is spreading the Mombachito story in central Iowa.

## Farmer-to-Farmer Program

Submitted photo

*Terry and Mary Hubers*

Terry Hubers, a truck driver for a farmers' coop, and his wife, Mary, a bookkeeper for a feed dealer, first traveled to Nicaragua to visit their daughter who was teaching in Managua. Their first response was culture shock.

"The country is like . . . oh, my word . . . " Mary paused, searching for words. "There was trash all over the city. The teachers picked us up in a clunky van with a back door that fell open every now and then. And they were talking and singing about how God is good all the time."

In 1997, the Hubers bought a few acres a mile or two west of Sioux Center, Iowa, moved a house and shed to the property, and bought some ponies. "I had my dream acreage with horses—everything I ever wanted," said Terry.

Then they started traveling to Nicaragua as part of the Farmer-to-Farmer program—a program of Partners Worldwide that encourages North American farmers to reach out to Nicaraguan farmers.  North America farmers help finance the purchase of land banks like Mombachito and make periodic visits to encourage the Nicaraguan farmers.

When the Hubers showed pictures of their home, the Nicaraguan farmers asked if it was a photo of a motel. It was so huge, they thought. "I felt about an inch tall," said Mary. "I came home and wondered how to pass that on to people. It is hard to explain if they haven't seen it."

She added, "I can't change the U.S., but can change my own priorities." They still live in the same house, but the horses are gone. "They weren't that important after all," said Terry. "They just made us busy, and there are other things to spend ourselves on."

And, over the years, their view of their Nicaragua trips has changed, too.  "The farmers are smart. They don't need our help. They know how to farm. Now I go every year to visit my friends Jennie and Maria Luisa," Mary said.

Yes, Jennie's house is a tenth the size of Mary's. It has a dirt floor. But the view out her kitchen door is magnificent. "You would have to pay a million dollars for it in the U.S.—and it is there just for her," exclaimed Mary. "When I step out her back kitchen, I think, 'Only God can do this, and it is here just for her.'"

The Hubers are an example of exactly what the Nehemiah Center has in mind: facilitating cultural exchanges to better understand biblical worldview and improve relationships.

At a dedication of a farmer's new coffee processing house, Mary and Jennie were asked to lead the prayer. "Jennie and I held hands and I prayed first [in English] and then she prayed [in Spanish]," said Mary. "It was special. Our friendship is special. And some day—though it hasn't happened on this earth—we will be able to talk directly with each other [without translators]."

Wendy Van Klinken, the former missionary who helped coordinate the Farmer-to-Farmer program, has witnessed these friendships many times, formed through annual visits and correspondence. "Even though they don't speak the same language or come from the same culture, there is such reciprocal love and education," said Wendy. "They pray for each other's loss of loved ones. When one of the Farmer-to-Farmer visitors was dying of lung cancer, the Mombachito farmers said to tell him they were praying for him. When he died, it was heartbreaking for them. He had become part of their family."

Hanging on the wall in the home of Bismark and Yasinia, a Mombachito farm couple, is a photo of Terry Hubers and other North Americans. Each evening before going to sleep, their son Jefferson blows a kiss toward the photos and says, "*Buenas noches.*"

## Materially Wealthy and Still Poor

The so-called elephant in the room is wealth—the clear disparities of material wealth that are so palpable to North Americans. The subject is a sensitive one, but one that is critical to face because of the often misguided desires by North Americans to share their wealth and the inability

*Iglesia Monte Horeb, Santa Matilde*

of North Americans to recognize their own poverty.

"Poverty is something we all have, and it is not just something financial," said Steve Holtrop.

Many of those associated with the Nehemiah Center have come to a better understanding of the nature of poverty and wealth from the book *When Helping Hurts: How to Alleviate Poverty Without Hurting the Poor and Yourself* by Steve Corbett and Brian Fikkert.

Poverty alleviation, according to Corbett and Fikkert, is "Moving people closer to glorifying God by living in right relationship with God, with self, with others, and with the rest of creation."[5]

The goal is not to turn the materially poor all over the world into wealthy citizens, a group often plagued by high rates of divorce, addictions, and mental illness. Nor is the goal only to make sure the materially poor simply have enough money.

Instead, the goal is to restore people to being what God created us all to be: People who glorify God by living in right relationship with God, self, others, and the rest of creation.

"Because every one of us is suffering from brokenness in our foundational relationships, all of us need 'poverty alleviation,' just in different ways," the authors write. "Our relationship to the materially poor should be one in which we recognize that both of us are broken and that both of us need the blessing of reconciliation. Our perspective should be less about how we are going to fix the materially poor and more about how we can walk together, asking God to fix both of us."[6]

Many of those associated with the Nehemiah Center grasp this concept with both hands.

"Why is it that billion-dollar poverty-alleviation programs don't work?" asked Eric Loftsgard. "There is no long-term transformational impact, no poverty alleviation. We need to address all four of those components; all four have to be part of poverty alleviation."

The model, he said, should become part of all cultures, including North America, which

---

[5] Steve Corbett and Brian Fikkert, *When Helping Hurts: How to Alleviate Poverty Without Hurting the Poor and Yourself,* Moody Publishers, Chicago, 2009. p. 78.

[6] Ibid., p. 79.

while not suffering from the same material poverty, suffers from self-poverty, other-poverty, and God-poverty. "We all have degrees of poverty. We all have issues within those four relational circles," said Eric.

"We are trying to instill this concept on a very introductory level into the groups that come here. It is not just about lacking the material things. All of our interventions have to address the whole person, and that means dealing with all of those four spheres."

What does that mean in the day-to-day lives of the short-term mission trippers? For one thing, it means North Americans cannot arrive in Nicaragua expecting to build something better than the native Nicaraguans. "Whenever you come into a situation and say, 'The way you made that chair—it works, but my chair is a lot better than your chair,' you have just destroyed that person," said Steve Holtrop.

That makes sense. Is it easy to do? No way. "If volunteers are like me, when they get off the plane, they are very cause-and-effect people," said former missionary David Van Klinken.

## A Lesson in Humility

In January 2000, Al Kopaska of Kellogg, Iowa, went on a mission trip with a group of men from his church to Nicaragua—farther than he'd ever been from home in his life. He attended all the informational meetings, listened to all the advice about not giving anything to the kids and watching his mannerisms.

But, one day, he was in a work group mixing concrete on the ground. You start with a pile of sand, then add cement and water to mix it. The volcano method, it is commonly called.

"I looked over in the corner, and there was an old Russian cement mixer," Al recalled. "I said to Andres, the maintenance supervisor, 'Why don't we use it?'"

"It doesn't run. Would you like to use it?"

"Yeah. I think I can fix it," Al told him.

"Long story short, I tried to fix it. I am a mechanic, and not afraid to tackle anything. It had a broken key drum and wouldn't turn. I worked all afternoon trying to take a bearing off. In Iowa, we use a cutting torch and replace the bearing. So I told Andres, 'I have to get that bearing off. I need a cutting torch.'"

"You have to save that bearing," Andres said.

"Why? What does a new bearing cost?"

"Seven dollars."

"Well, let's go buy one. I spent more than that just talking here."

Joel Huyser and Greg Kynast, at that time the director of Nicaragua Christian Academy, had listened to Al's conversation. "One of them said to me 'You goofed up. The man who was standing next to you makes two dollars a day. That is three days' wages.'"

In retelling the story, Al held up his thumb and first finger. "I felt this high."

"They are here because they are going to do something, change the situation," said Wendy, David's wife. "It has been our desire to share the bigger picture with short-term teams . . . the holistic view of missions. You are part, but this is what goes on the rest of the year in that person's life when you are not here."

Nor can North Americans approach missions as a way of offering handouts.

"The big thing I have learned here is that God's desire for holistic transformation is not just for the poor but wealthy as well," said Andrea Kamouyerou, former FH team coordinator. "How we view ourselves has to be an honest assessment based on Scripture.

"We don't want to further impoverish Nicaraguans by giving something they could do themselves. That way we are teaching them they can't do for themselves. A lot of organizations have handed out, handed down. That is a broken identity . . . We talk a lot about good stewardship. That levels the playing field. Whether wealthy or poor, all are called to stewardship," said Andrea.

North American visitors would love to give things to the Nicaragua farmers, but Wendy and David Van Klinken adamantly maintained their policies of no-handouts for the farmers. "We don't *give* them anything. Not one bean. Not one machete," said David.

"We have seen aid develop dependency," he added. "So, all financial aid is channeled through the Nicaraguan national organizations." Even the Farm Bureau T-shirts that North Americans brought to farmers of La Dahlia needed to be earned. They were given as awards for attending an educational meeting—they became an incentive for change.

After Hurricane Mitch, relief flooded into the town of Dario. Agencies came and built houses for people. "When another hurricane was predicted, I heard with my own ears someone in that town say 'I hope it hits hard so we can get new houses,'" David said.

Yet the line can be difficult to draw.

"Up on the farms, we don't give them anything. Not one bean," repeated Wendy. "Yet when there is a death in the family on the farm, the North American affiliate, through us, brings the family a bag of rice, beans, and cooking oil, because they are expected to feed everyone at the funeral. That is disaster relief. You become that bread of life that God expects of us."

Focus too long on relief, and you create dependency. Focus too much on economic sustainability, and you may forget God's call for compassion. "How you meld those two is a difficult thing at times," Wendy acknowledged. "Sometimes we have bad days. Some days I miss the hundred percent compassion of relief in medical missions. What we do now is so much harder than that.

"You have to have a balance. We at the Nehemiah Center try to find balance."

To be clear, North American missionaries aren't ignoring the reality that many Nicaraguans are, in fact, materially poor. On the contrary, understanding what that really means may be part of a service-and-learning team's experience. The Van Klinkens shared how a Canadian team learned a real lesson from Mombachito farmers:

Service-and-learning team member Jean De Waard and team coordinator Alma Hernández paint a hand-powered water pump in Santa Lucia.

Work team members from Ponoka, Alberta, Canada, spent the day picking coffee alongside Mombachito farmers. Together, they all strapped on their *canastas* (baskets) and picked beans. They filled three-quarters of a hundred-pound bag. After lunch, the Mombachito farmers walked the Canadian farmers through the rest of the process—depulping, washing, and drying the beans.

At the end of the day, the Mombachito farmers said to the Canadians: "This is what you will be paid today because you didn't work very hard. You only got a quarter of a basket of beans each."

Altogether the Canadians were paid about $5 for the half-day's work of eight people. When the Canadians added up their bills for hotel, breakfast, lunch, and dinner, they discovered they would pay fifty times more than what they earned.

"To some a lot is given and a lot is expected of you. Wherever you are, whatever your circumstances, God expects you to be giving in some way," said Wendy. "To chastise people for having riches is wrong. People do different things with what they have. And if God hasn't touched their hearts with how to give, no one should judge them.

"Poverty, middle class, wealth—these are not economic levels but mentality levels. These farmers are not considering themselves in poverty. They talk about what they have, not about what they don't have. 'I'm going to make my house better; I'm going to raise more vegetables.' They see themselves as middle class," Wendy added.

Added translator Rolando Mejía: "All that you have belongs to the Lord, and until you understand that, you go nowhere."

This principle is important to all Nehemiah Center partners: For disaster you provide relief; you give away the essentials to sustain life. But for development, you avoid creating economic dependence. You walk alongside the people to assist them in achieving independence.

Anyone not yet convinced of this principle should consider for a moment what could happen if money to alleviate poverty were to simply fall out of the sky. The results can be disastrous.

In his regular newsletter to donors, Mark VanderWees, a missionary with CRWRC, shared a heartbreaking story about the village of Wiwinak, a community of about eight hundred people about eighty kilometers from the nearest road, electricity, or police officer. The CRWRC and its Nicaraguan partner Accion Medica Cristiana (AMC) had been working there for four years, promoting preventative health, sustainable agriculture, and disaster risk management.

The situation in Wiwinak changed drastically when a small plane crashed in the village, carrying a cargo of cocaine and money. The crew didn't survive, but the money apparently was distributed among the villagers and those of three nearby communities. The cocaine probably was converted to cash by reselling it to drug traffickers. As Mark told the story:

*Service-and-learning team member Stan Heersink prepares lunch with Tesoros de Dios cooks.*

> Overnight, the community was transformed, but not in the way we had anticipated. Merchants from the closest town . . . descended on Wiwinak, bringing with them all kinds of products for sale, from clothing to generators to chainsaws. Whereas before I would have had a hard time buying a pencil in a barter-based economy, now DVD players can be purchased for cash.

> Armed robbers moved into the town. Though it was planting time, the community showed little motivation to work.

What happened to the leadership training we invested in Wiwinak? Why didn't the authorities intervene? In a conversation with Francisco Gutiérrez, the [former] director of AMC, he shared that it was "painstakingly clear that unless there is an underlying Biblical world view, our community development efforts are in vain."[7]

Making a transformation, coming to understand a biblical worldview, takes years, lifetimes, to accomplish, if it ever is. It's a journey, and clearly the Wiwinak people hadn't progressed far enough on their journey to successfully meet the challenge they faced. The journey isn't always straightforward; sometimes there will be steps backward.

The goal, however, for the Nehemiah Center is to start people on that journey—people in Wiwinak, people in El Limonal, people in Mombachito, people in Alberta, Canada, people in Sioux Center, Iowa, and people in Sunnyside, Washington.

Consider the distance already traveled by this short-termer, whose comments Andrea relates here: "I have always thought that God blessed me materially, and not only do I no longer think that—because I understand there are different ways that God blesses—but I also see my material possessions as something that inhibits my relationship with God. Maybe my possessions and culture are buffering me from dependence on the Lord."

Transformation starts in the individual and grows. Once transformation takes hold, only then can it lead to transformations in marriages, families, churches, communities, and more.

---

[7] Mark VanderWees, "News from Nicaragua," CRWRC newsletter, December 2009.

*Transporting water from an area stream*

# 06

## Fish Pancakes

*We used to see things as either "secular" or "spiritual." Now we see that everything is from God and for God.*

*- ALEJANDRO ESPINOZA, PASTOR, IGLESIA GETSEMANÍ ASAMBLEA DE DIOS*

*(GETSEMANÍ CHURCH, ASSEMBLY OF GOD) IN LEÓN*

At twenty-five, Lourdes Rivas, a pastor's wife and mother of two, walked along a León river reflecting on her marriage. She looked at her wedding band and remembered that she hadn't received it from her husband, Alejandro Espinoza.[1] She had purchased it herself. She tugged it from her finger and flung it into the muddy water.

*Lourdes Rivas*

At fourteen, she had been attracted to her congregation's new bachelor pastor. She flirted, he responded, and a year later when she completed fourth grade, they married. Within two years, they had two daughters. The first delivery had been terrifying. Arecely was delivered by Alejandro because a 1988 hurricane made it impossible to get to a midwife or health center. The second delivery was lonely—Maybelline was born in a hospital, with Alejandro miles away.

The four of them lived in a Sunday school room of Getsemaní church in León, with little space and less privacy. Members of the congregation pushed aside the doorway curtain and entered without knocking, sometimes while Lourdes was dressing for the day. With a low ceiling and little

---

[1]In formal situations in Nicaragua, as in many Latin American countries, both men and women typically use their first name, followed by their father's last name, and then their mother's last name. Informally, both men and women usually drop their mother's last name. Only sometimes do married women take on their husband's name—when they do they typically add "de" and then follow it with their husband's first surname.

air circulation, it was usually stiflingly hot.

Lourdes longed for a house for her family, but she had no idea how much Alejandro earned. She hadn't completed high school, and she was unable to contribute to the family income. She did know that their income was meager. Each month they bought groceries and supplies on credit, and then paid as much of that bill as they were able on payday.

One of ten children, Lourdes had grown up in a poor family in a rural area of León. At ten, Lourdes started school, where she was mocked for lacking shoes and having big feet. Low self-esteem sent down deep roots—along with a capacity for violence. Older and larger than other students in class, she sometimes resorted to overturning their drinks, hitting them, and even once deposited a classmate in a pile of cow dung.

She was an abuser, but also a victim. Her mother beat her almost daily with ropes and other objects, and sometimes tied her to a tree. The severity of the beating was determined by how angry her mother was or how significant she thought Lourdes' misconduct. Her mother told Lourdes that pigs had more value than she did: at least a pig could be sold for money. In the rural village, daily worship and daily beatings were a typical part of a child's life.

As Lourdes entered adulthood, her violent streak continued. She once spanked her daughter, fifteen, so hard, the daughter became teary-eyed thereafter whenever Lourdes came near her. Although Lourdes was never physically abused by Alejandro, she didn't count on his respect in her marriage, nor had she seen or experienced it.

When she attended meetings with other pastors' wives, Lourdes looked like a typical *señora del campo* (peasant woman). Shy and withdrawn, she paid little attention to grooming—and at one of the meetings she overheard derogatory comments about her appearance. When seated, she hid her feet under her skirt or tucked them beneath her chair.

## Marriages in Trouble

Across Nicaragua, marriages are troubled. A culture of *machismo* still dominates, which means that women frequently have a lower education than men, and if they have a job, it most often pays less than what their husbands earn. It is not uncommon for a husband to have women on the side. As Lourdes explained, "The man is the boss. He is the one who has the money at home, and he has the power in the house and makes the decisions. The woman depends on him."

Domestic violence is common: forty-eight percent of married or partnered women report having received verbal or psychological abuse. Almost one in three Nicaraguan women reports having experienced physical or sexual violence. Often abuse is also directed toward youth and adolescents in family settings.[2]

---

[2]"Domestic Violence Prevention and Awareness-Raising in Nicaragua," CRWRC Justice Grant Proposal, Feb. 2010, quoting statistics from the Preliminary Report of the Nicaraguan Demographics and Health Survey.

Laws exist that are designed to protect women, children, and adolescents from violence, but the reality is that violence in the country continues to increase.

Though one might think that the families of pastors would buck this trend, in truth, these marriages aren't notably different. The difference, perhaps, is that their marital problems also affect the church, for multiple reasons. The most apparent reason is that the leadership style a male pastor exercises in his home naturally carries over into the leadership style he practices in the church and community. If he is a dictator at home, he has difficulty being a servant leader in the church and community.

Too often, pastors don't consider their marriages important in their relationship with God, according to Luz López, a psychologist and the Ezra team coordinator at the Nehemiah Center. "They are not interested in resolving family problems or in the economic well-being of their family."

When wives complain, as Lourdes did, about the lack of a family home, the pastors think their wives aren't very spiritual for wanting to have their own house, Luz said. Nor is education for the wives important. "They can't communicate with each other, and they try to resolve everything by praying or fasting, and do not take time to talk and identify the problems," said Luz.

Problems are exacerbated by financial concerns as well. "Many have problems buying food for the family because many of the pastors depend just on the collection plate on Sunday. If there is no money, there is no food in the pastor's family that week," added Luz.

"They cannot help other members of the church because they have not resolved their own problems."

## Discovering God's Model for Marriage

In 2001, Lourdes and Alejandro heard about a marriage course the Nehemiah Center was offering to pastoral couples—a training that required the attendance of both the pastor and his wife. "I was excited when they said we had to attend together," said Lourdes. The course was taught by a husband-wife psychologist team, Manuel Largaespada and Luz López.

The ten-session course entitled "Manual for Marriage: Restoring the Original Model" included such topics as the original model and purpose for marriage and the role of both men and women in developing the world God created. With that foundation in place, the course covered practical application of this worldview in family finances, sex, rearing children, decision-making, communication, and more. The course concluded with an invitation to the pastors and their wives to multiply the blessing by sharing the model with others.

*Luz López*

Luz, a skilled teacher, began drawing Lourdes from her shell. "In classes, Luz would ask me, 'Lourdes, what do you think?' and I could give my opinion. I don't know if I said the right things, but she always said, 'Excellent. Do you want to say anything else?' I started to gain trust in myself. I thought, 'I *can* say things that are right and good.'"

Lourdes and Alejandro improved their family communication. They agreed to two marriage guidelines: They would not go to bed angry with each other, and they would try not to say things that would hurt each other.

---

## Nehemiah Center Training Hits Many Fronts

Fostering healthy marriages and growing healthy churches are two core training focuses for the Nehemiah Center—the building blocks, as center founder Joel Huyser called them. Fostering healthy communities, strengthening Christian schools, and equipping churches to reach youth at risk are other core efforts for the Nehemiah Center covered in later chapters. In addition, the Nehemiah Center assists in some way with a variety of other programs.

One of those additional programs is *Buen Trato* (Healthy Relationships). This program, coordinated by Lourdes Rivas, is a response to the widespread presence of domestic violence in Nicaraguan society, including evangelicals. Buen Trato focuses on forming healthy relationships of mutual respect between women and men. Lourdes works with fifty different churches and has trained about three hundred leaders in León, Chinandega, and El Viejo. Partnering with other Christian organizations, the program has also reached couples in Boaco and Jinotepe.

As Lourdes explained it, the program covers eight topics and is meant to be taught to the entire family, not just the women. It helps couples understand healthy and unhealthy relationships, the cycles of abuse and the consequences. It also discusses interior healing, conflict resolution, child protection, trauma, and parenting. Practical exercises so that the couples learn to adapt these messages to their own situations are an integral part of the training.

Another program developed by the center to improve families is an effort to raise HIV/AIDS awareness. (Both are funded through the Christian Reformed World Relief Committee.) In 2003, one case of HIV/AIDS was reported a week in the country. By 2007, that number increased to one reported case per day. In 2007, the Nehemiah Center piloted a program to educate and involve local churches in addressing the problem. The program's focus is to strengthen the capability of the local church and community organizations to respond in a holistic way to people living with HIV/AIDS and to serve as facilitators of education and outreach about the disease.

The Ezra staff of the Nehemiah Center has also helped Christian Reformed World Relief Committee (CRWRC) facilitate workshops for its other Nicaraguan partners, such as the Christian Center for Human Rights, in such areas as biblical worldview, methods of adult education, and transformational development. Almost every week there is a training session at the Nehemiah Center, and often there are multiple trainings at the same time. For instance, early in 2011, Food for the Hungry and CRWRC jointly sponsored a two-day agricultural conference that brought in eighty Nicaraguan farmers to discuss worldview and agriculture.

Lourdes learned that Alejandro had been so terrified during the difficult birth of their first daughter that he had been afraid to accompany her to the second birth. She asked her daughter's forgiveness for the beating. Eventually she even told her mother she had forgiven her for the beatings of her childhood. "My mother was puzzled by it," she remembered. "She said she hadn't treated me any differently from any of my brothers and sisters."

*Alejandro Espinoza and Lourdes Rivas*

In time, the couple also began to think differently about Lourdes' potential. Alejandro encouraged her to complete her high school education and pursue advanced degrees. She and Alejandro now both have theology degrees, and Alejandro cared for their daughters while Lourdes completed a degree in psychology.

Asked how their handling of finances changed, Alejandro requested Lourdes' permission to take the lead on this answer. She nodded, leaned back with her hands clasped behind her, her feet extended and clearly visible.

Alejandro, seated on the couch in their colorful living room, spoke with the resonant and careful articulation of a long-term pastor as he described their previous practice of buying supplies on credit from a local store, and then falling short on that debt on payday in a vicious and repeating cycle. They agreed to pay off the store, buying only what they had cash for, carefully evaluating their needs and creating an opportunity to save. They also asked the church treasurer to remove ten percent of their wages before paying them, to ensure consistent tithing. "That helped a lot, because I was giving to the Lord," Alejandro said.

With her psychology degree, Lourdes found employment. "When I saw the Nehemiah Center people doing trainings, I wished I were one of them," said Lourdes. "I never told anyone." Then one day, she received a telephone call asking if she would lead *Buen Trato* (a paraphrased translation is "Healthy Relationships"), the new domestic violence program that the Nehemiah Center was starting. Equipped with self-esteem, teaching skills, and a degree, she readily agreed. She works part-time for that program and part-time as a counselor at Villa Esperanza, a home for orphaned girls.

Alejandro summarizes the marriage seminar impact on their own marriage as three-pronged: 1) They learned how to be a good husband and wife. 2) They learned how to be better stewards of their financial resources. 3) They learned that their life for God is not just church work; instead, jobs, careers—their whole lives—are guided by the Bible.

Since 2001, Alejandro and Lourdes have attended many more Nehemiah Center-sponsored seminars, and their vision has grown. Getsemaní church has expanded its outreach to the community through home groups, special couples' nights for parents, a women's sewing program, and biblical counseling services. Its congregation hosts a Healthy Church training program for León-area congregations. "We used to be isolated from the community, but now the community sees we are interested in them," said Lourdes.

With much prayer, employment for Lourdes, a family budget, and time, Lourdes and Alejandro were able to purchase a home. It has a high ceiling, cross-ventilation, and colorful walls—even by Nicaraguan standards—each one painted in a bright blue, red, or gold. The walls display their diplomas and photos of their daughters' *quinceañeras* (fifteenth birthday parties).

By 2010, Lourdes had become a gracious and self-assured hostess. With the help of a sister and niece, she provided dinner for a twelve-member North American service-and-learning team and then told them about her life and work. Her hair was carefully tied back. She wore a pendant, earrings—and a gold wedding ring. She wears the gold ring at home and other safe places, she explained. When she travels alone on the bus to work in Managua, in case of theft, she wears a cheaper silver one.

These wedding bands—both of them—were purchased by her husband.

## Making Fish Pancakes

*Luz López and Manuel Largaespada*

The Nehemiah Center's focus on healthy relationships came about, like the center itself, after that first 1999 conference on biblical worldview. In the year or so after the paradigm-shattering conference in Managua, subsequent worldview conferences for pastors were sponsored in other parts of Nicaragua with less success. "We did not feel we were hitting home," said Joel Huyser. "In Spanish, we were *pescando sin anzuelo*. (We were fishing without a hook.)"

Manuel and Luz suggested a change: conferences that focused on pastoral marriages and families.

Manuel made their case with an illustration from his family. His Scandinavian brother-in-law wanted his daughters to eat fish, but they refused: they hated fish. However, they loved pancakes. So, he created fish pancakes, and the children devoured them, getting both what they wanted and what they needed. "Teaching worldview through theological concepts is fish," he said. "If we teach it through practical marriage topics, we will have fish pancakes."

As psychologists, Manuel and Luz saw the brokenness in pastoral marriages as a high need.

"Only men attended the pastoral worldview conferences, and we thought many marriage difficulties were the result of wives being in the background—in the church and everywhere else," said Manuel. "A sense of justice was needed in which both grew together, helping each other.

"In the marriage workshops we started in 2001, we did something strange. I taught for an hour; then Luz taught for an hour." He smiled and added, "One of the best talents God gave Luz was teaching. That made the pastors notice that the seminars were better because she was teaching with me!"

Manuel said, "I think we were able to gain their [the participants'] trust and respect because we opened up our own lives." In the first three years of their marriage, Luz and Manuel had moved twelve times, a cause of marital stress. Finally, together they decided to buy their current home. When they talked to classes about finances, they told of their own practice—neither of them spends more than ten dollars without checking with the other—a revolutionary practice for the pastors in their classes, Luz said.

A first requirement for the pastoral marriage seminars was the attendance and participation of both spouses. "We found that the best way to bring a pastor's focus to the real world and real life, instead of being animistic and focused purely on the spiritual, was through his family," said Manuel.

Pastor Thomas Aquino of León is a dramatic example of that switch. One day he traveled to a distant congregation and preached, as he frequently did, that it didn't matter if there was no electricity, no food, no water, because Christ is the light of the world and the bread of life. When he hitchhiked home—he had no money for transportation—he discovered his electricity and water cut off. He had not been paid for the out-of-town preaching engagement, so there would be no food either. Through the marriage workshops, he came to realize that physical life is important. He started a small side business, selling construction blocks, to supplement his income. He no longer preaches these things are unimportant. He and his wife took the marriage seminar series twice, and then they began to teach the series to others.

Another pastor, Pastor Abel Rostran, president of his area pastors' association, attended the workshops with his wife and subsequently invited Luz and Manuel to kick off a marriage seminar he started in his own congregation. Ready to start the first session, Luz and Manuel didn't see his wife. They asked the pastor where she was. "In the kitchen preparing food," he replied. They told him they could not begin class without her. She was fetched and class began.

Luz and Manuel learned she was unable to read and wasn't comfortable in leadership at teaching events. Over the next few years she learned to read and joined her husband in teaching. They now have an unusually strong marriage ministry—they trained five other couples to help lead and draw seventy to eighty couples to their seminars. Their congregation has since launched other programs such as a program with Compassion International (a Christian child advocacy ministry) along with an elementary and a secondary school.

Luz and Manuel developed another curriculum called "Mentoring in Counseling" to help pastors and wives counsel other people. The program covers five sessions spread over a year. After going through that training, the pastoral couples often feel more comfortable counseling others. Some churches that established marriage ministry programs discover they can reach more couples by offering couples' nights—meals in a romantic setting with a special talk on a theme involving the marriage relationship. These couples' nights have been especially promising because they attract the men who otherwise skip all church functions. And sometimes, these nights lead the men back to the church.

Subsequent to creating the marriage workshops, Luz and Manuel have moved on to other roles. Luz, an excellent writer, creates workshop manuals for the Nehemiah Center and now heads the center's Ezra team. Manuel left the Nehemiah Center in 2003 to work with the Nicaragua Bible League, which he volunteered to leave in 2010 because of budget cuts. He is planting a church and helping Luz with her work. The marriage training continues under the leadership of Alejandro and Lourdes and other couples who have experienced dramatic change in their own marriage relationship.

## Transformed to Transform Others

With the help of Luz and Manuel, the Nehemiah Center's influence grew as those involved realized that it was important not just to teach biblical worldview as an abstract concept, but also to apply biblical principles to the real-life problems people were facing. As previously mentioned, it was initially the need to heal broken marriages that led leaders to more fully grasp the concept that biblical worldview was something to be lived and demonstrated—not just taught. Because leaders at the Nehemiah Center recognized that biblical worldview encompassed marriages, people like Lourdes and Alejandro changed their lives and started impacting other lives around them.

This theme echoes that of earlier chapters: progressive transformation. Luz and Manuel became agents of transformation for Lourdes and Alejandro. That was the first step. By transforming themselves, Lourdes and Alejandro have assimilated the principles of biblical worldview into their lives and have become agents of transformation themselves.

## Healthy Churches

By nine o'clock Sunday morning at *Iglesia Cristiana Verbo* (Verbo Christian Church), seven hundred people are inside singing, clapping, and tapping their feet to songs of praise and longing for their Lord. Their joyful noise along with the sounds of the keyboards, drum, and guitar bounce sounds off the green walls. Some arms are upraised swaying to the beat. Some heads are bowed to the words.

An hour later, the songs give way to announcements. First-time visitors are applauded; ushers move to welcome each one.

Finally, the pastor, clearly well educated and knowledgeable about the Bible, begins his message, first with a couple Bible readings, then with a sermon in typical roundabout Nicaraguan fashion. He approaches his subject matter like a chicken roasting on a rotisserie, repeating his theme in multiple ways with multiple examples.

A wonderful church. Dynamic. Welcoming. Passionate about serving its members, visitors, and the community around it.

Exceptional? Yes.

The truth is that Nicaragua has many churches, but few are dynamic. The country has many pastors, but few are trained.

Churches desperately need additional training, according to Henry Cruz, himself a pastor of a Four Square congregation in Managua. An Ezra team member, Henry leads the *Fortalecimiento Eclesial* (FE) program for the Nehemiah Center. The Spanish term literally means Church Strengthening, but in English, the program generally is called the Healthy Church program. The Nehemiah Center began

*Sunday morning worship at Iglesia Cristiana Verbo*

*Front entry to Iglesia Cristiana Verbo*

the program in 2008, and after much research and thought, has developed eight manuals it uses in the trainings.

Churches in Chinandega, León, Managua, and Granada have enrolled in the program, and about two dozen churches from these areas were taking part in the trainings in 2011. In addition, another sixteen churches enrolled from the Esteli area (a new region of focus that is discussed in more depth in Chapter 10).

Nicaraguan churches have far more problems than those directly stemming from low pastor salaries. Few churches have any contact with their communities outside of evangelistic crusades, and seventy percent of pastors have no theological training. In many churches, women make up

*Henry Cruz*

well over two-thirds of those who attend. The average church has about 130 members, though some have only a couple dozen.

The lack of what Henry calls integral evangelism is a huge concern. Some churches may practice what they consider to be evangelism, but not integral evangelism. "Integral evangelism has two big themes: proclamation and demonstration," said Henry. "We only proclaim, but we don't demonstrate. That is evangelism, but not integral evangelism. We want integral evangelism. It is very weak here."

Henry also sees a multitude of other problems: a weak understanding of the mission, no strategic plan, no access to training, an authoritarian rather than a servant leadership model, no healthy growth. The list goes on.

Just as it had realized that pastors' marriages had to be healed and transformed before pastors could effectively lead their churches, the Nehemiah Center came to see that churches themselves needed to be healthy before they could effectively launch programs for their communities.

"Just as a pastor who did not view his wife as an equal partner in the Lord could not be a servant leader in his church, so a church that was not healthy could not transform its community," said Joel Huyser. "So three years ago we began to focus on church health as an essential building block for effective and sustainable community transformation.

"FE has become the essential building block for our work with churches."

FE trainers work with churches over a ten-month period, covering a manual each month through a participative study. Church pastors and the church leaders discuss topics such as expository preaching, biblical worldview, and servant leadership; liturgy and worship (understanding the role music, for example, should play in worship); and integral evangelism (how their church can become part of the community).

Churches who take part in the training also have harder work to do: diagnosing and evaluating their own church and administration, working on strategic planning, and developing an action plan.

As Joel said, this training is a building block. This building block has led:

- A Chinandega church to start working with ten prostitutes, teaching them handicrafts such as making piñatas while also teaching them about God's plan of salvation. "This church is saying Jesus loves you and helping them find economic solutions as well. This is integral evangelism," said Henry. "Before this training, that would have been a population segment that this church would not get near."
- Churches to step into their communities by forming youth baseball teams in order to attract youth.
- Pastor Alejandro Espinoza (mentioned earlier in this chapter) to organize a praise min-

istry and also expand his ministry to jails. The church has a team of ten men who visit the jail once a month to bring personal items and to evangelize.

- Churches to expand their vision of what is possible. In Santa Matilde, a pastor smiled as he said that some area residents refer to him as "that crazy pastor" because of his vision for the future, which includes a market and a pharmacy in the community.

- Churches to strengthen themselves so that they can successfully launch other programs to help their communities.

*Typical rural church building in Santa Lucia area, which later became a pastor's home when the congregation outgrew this space.*

The *Amor Viviente* (literally, Living Love) church in Chinandega, for example, has hosted marital counseling programs, programs for people with terminal disease, and training to raise awareness for HIV/AIDS. It regularly works with youth at risk and has launched a Community Health Evangelism (CHE) program. Its pastor, Porfirio Maldonado, said the FE training has also made him more aware of the importance of administrative structure, accountability, and budgeting.

The result of these programs? A country helping itself to transform. The Nehemiah Center's Ezra team—all Nicaraguans—train the local leaders. Once the local leaders grasp the concepts—grasp the change biblical worldview makes in their own lives—the transformation spreads. It happens one step at a time. One building block at a time. One person at a time.

## Taking the Steps:
## Transforming a Marriage, a Church, a Community, a Nation

The story of Daniel Boniche and his wife, Gloria Saballos, is similar to that of Lourdes and Alejandro in that they, too, experienced brokenness in their marriage. At one point in their lives, the couple even divorced—Gloria, vowing to God that she wouldn't do anything to help God's church; and Daniel, turning to alcohol and other women in futile attempts to eliminate his anger.

How their lives were turned around is a story of personal transformation. What they are doing now with their lives—Daniel Boniche is the Nehemiah Center's executive director and Gloria Saballos is a leader in many church and school programs—is a story of transformation with an impact that is spreading across their country.

Born in 1955, Daniel grew up in a relatively stable family. His father, a bricklayer, and his

*Daniel Boniche and Gloria Saballos with their daughter, Irene (center)*

mother, a housewife, were married fifty years before her death a few years ago. For most of his life, he attended evangelical churches.

A man who smiles easily with a collection of anecdotes and punch lines on call, Daniel must have been a spunky kid. Considered to be from the wrong neighborhood, in elementary school Daniel became a target of bullies. "I was short. Skinny. I was not seen as strong," he said. "So, I learned to run very well." As protection, he made friends with a strong, mentally disabled boy who, at Daniel's urging, put one of Daniel's tormentors down a well for three hours. That boy never went after Daniel again.

Once, when some boys fell into a water fountain near the school during a fight, the school's director became angry. "He made us stand like a statue in the entry to the school. We had to stand with heavy books in our hands with one leg raised behind us." Another time, after Daniel had repeatedly refused to sing the national anthem of Nicaragua, the school director put him in the middle of the patio. "They took everyone out of school to hear me sing the national anthem as a solo. I had to do it, or I would have been kicked out of school."

As he grew older, his education was better than that of many Nicaraguans, but that streak of independence continued. In the age of the hippies, he grew his hair long and wore a big medal. On his feet, he wore sandals made of tires. As a student prior to the 1979 revolution, he burned Somoza's soldiers in effigy. "On the bridge by the university, I would put effigies of soldiers. As guards were coming down the street, I would set these on fire and run before I could be caught."

In 1980, a year after the Sandinistas took control of the government, Daniel became part of the Sandinistas' literacy campaign, put into a significant leadership position for the first time in what turned out to be a successful effort to improve literacy in the country.

By 1982, he graduated as a civil engineer and subsequently studied in Spain where he obtained master's degrees in hydraulic engineering and water engineering. Within a couple years, he married Gloria, and they were blessed by the birth of their son, Maxdiel.

However, in the early 1990s, the couple was hit hard by the misfortune that changed their lives: they lost a child. When the little girl, Ibet Sofia, was born, doctors told them she had a defective heart and would live only three days. In fact, she lived for seven months before she died.

"After that, I didn't have a love for anything," said Gloria. "Then we started to grow apart from each other because Daniel was also in pain but could not let it out. We thought as the world thinks, that we didn't love each other. When the judge asked us why we wanted to divorce, neither of us knew. It was just pride. We just did it for selfishness. And we were just mad. We wanted to punish God. We wanted to turn our backs on him."

In their own ways, both did just that. Gloria vowed to God: "I will go to the church and sit in the last bench and not kneel or go up front, not work in anything, until you let me understand if there was a purpose with the death of my daughter."

After she had made that vow, she thought of her brother, who had turned his back on God years earlier. She told God that if the death of her daughter had a purpose, then let her brother stand in church and be reconciled. She never thought it would happen.

It was quite a surprise to her when, from her seat on the last bench in the church, she saw

## Improving Literacy, the Sandinista Way

Following the 1979 revolution during which they gained control of the government, the Sandinistas launched the National Literacy Crusade of 1980 that by most accounts made significant inroads toward educating the largely illiterate country. Daniel Boniche was about twenty-five years old and still at the university when he was put in charge of six literacy brigades, each of which had thirty people. "All the training was almost like the military, the way it was run," Daniel said. Essentially, the program recruited literate young people, often from the cities and sent them out to remote areas to teach. Schools were closed that year from March through August. More than sixty thousand high school and college students were sent throughout the country. Another twenty-five thousand worked in the cities to teach anyone over ten years old who could not read or write.[1]

"Whether you were for or against the Sandinistas—everyone will say the literacy campaign was one of the best things the Sandinistas did," said Daniel. "Illiteracy went from forty-eight to twelve percent. They had songs they sang. It was an incredible motivational effort." Many students from the city, who knew nothing of the peasant life, lived with and worked among the poor families. "Many of these relationships lasted a long time. It was not uncommon for these people to talk about their family in the city and their family in the rural area. Some of the rural families later would send their kids to study, and they would stay with the family of their teacher in the city," said Daniel.

At the end of the campaign, one of Daniel's duties was to move youth who had been working in the mountains back to Managua. "I had to look for transportation, boats, food, for twenty thousand. The whole northern Atlantic was my territory . . . It was my first administrative responsibility."

---

[1]Thomas Walker. *Nicaragua: Living in the Shadow of the Eagle,* Westview Press, Boulder, Colorado, 2003, p. 124.

her brother walk in the door. He told the congregation he wanted to reconcile with God because his heart was moved by seeing his sister lose her child.

"When I saw this, something broke inside of me, like chains around my heart," Gloria recalled. "I kneeled in that same place, and started crying and crying, and asked the Lord to forgive me for my rebellion. And there, the Lord broke all the negative things in my life and started to restore all. Family and neighbors gave testimony that because of the death of my child, their hearts were touched. Today, they are leaders in our church."

Meanwhile, during this time, Daniel led a life on the margin. Having left the family home, he stayed with his parents, with his friends, at the properties of places he worked. He lived a life he wasn't proud of. "I was totally away—from God, family, everything, and I was very confused," said Daniel.

One day, a friend, Roger Leyton, stopped him on the road. Knowing that Daniel was an engineer, Roger asked Daniel to look at his home because he needed advice about a structural problem.

As Daniel approached Roger's house the next day, he thought it strange that such a nice home would have a serious structural problem. Roger led him inside and showed him a two-inch-long crack in the wall.

"When I saw this, I thought, 'He is making fun of me.'"

"He said, 'Sit down. Let's talk. I know that you understand now that the structural problem was just a way to make you come here, but the Lord wants to restore your life.'

"And he gave me a challenge: 'If you have the interest in God restoring your life, you can stay in this home until the Lord restores you. But you have to make that decision.'

"And obviously, I did want the Lord to restore my life. I saw everything so dark. No possibilities."

Daniel stayed with his friend. Roger and other pastors spent several days talking with Daniel. "They made me fast . . . and I would talk about everything that had happened. They would listen as I talked and talked and talked. They would put their hands on me and pray. And there were four days of this until from my voice came a request of forgiveness to God."

Through Roger, Daniel became reunited with Gloria. The couple spent a lot of time talking, and on April 27, 1994, they got married again in the same church as the first time.

And despite being told that she couldn't have any more children, Gloria gave birth to a healthy girl, Irene. "She has become a counsel as a sign of everything, because God restored our marriage so now we can help others and reach more souls for the Lord," said Gloria.

"And this is why I tell people we have two children, one from each marriage," Daniel said with a grin.

The couple uses this story frequently as they counsel other couples with troubled marriages. "There is a great need for Christians to get involved with each other's marriages," said Gloria. "It takes time," she added. "We had a process of interior restoring of health where the Lord took us step-by-step, seeing the hidden things we had in our heart and healing us."

As the family reconciled, Daniel continued to support his family as an engineer. The couple wanted nothing to do with the job of a pastor, but at the same time they considered it important to support their pastor. They had many responsibilities at the church, and when their pastor was gone, he would leave Daniel in charge. When the pastor resigned, church members asked Daniel to become pastor. That was twelve years ago, and the couple today continues as co-pastors.

However, this wasn't all that God had in store for Daniel and Gloria. Now that their marriage was healed, God started revealing to them his additional plans. Various connections, primarily through another couple they had counseled, gradually led Daniel and Gloria to the Nehemiah Center.

"I began to learn about biblical worldview," said Daniel. "As I learned about it, I sensed it was something I had felt all my life without realizing it."

It was around the year 2000 that he began working half-time for the Nehemiah Center.

It seemed to be a good fit—partly because of Daniel's capacity to develop other leaders. "My first years as a pastor, I worked at raising up other leadership in the church. I have always seen my primary task to build the capacity of new leaders within the church. One thing I have always practiced is to give other people the freedom to do things. When people come to me with ideas, I make a few modifications and say run with it."

That attitude is different from the practice of many Nicaraguan pastors. Daniel and Gloria delegate responsibilities to leaders within their congregation. "I have learned to trust what God does through different people," Daniel said. "The leaders are responsible for their own tasks, and they do them better than I could."

That same approach has worked well in Daniel's association with the Nehemiah Center. "Daniel has special characteristics," said Joel Huyser. "He is not looking out for his own interests. He has the ability to let things go and develop other leaders."

With Daniel becoming more involved with the Ezra team, Joel stepped out of his management of the Ezra team in 2004. And, by July 2008, Joel formally stepped away as the Nehemiah Center's executive director. Daniel Boniche became the center's first Nicaraguan executive director.

Indeed, healing their marriage was just a first step in God's plan for this couple.

Today, Daniel and Gloria live in Sector Oriental, a Managua neighborhood about twenty-five to forty-five minutes away from the Nehemiah Center, depending on traffic. They continue to serve as pastors of the *Centro de Fe y Vida Nueva* (Center of Faith and New Life) in the Maria Auxiliadora barrio. Their church now includes a school with twenty-two teachers and three hundred students in preschool, elementary, and high school grades. The church itself has an active leadership, with 14 deacons, 2 lifelong deacons, and 350 active members. The church has spawned three daughter churches.

FROM CAROL'S JOURNAL

## *A Special Place*

*Gloria Saballos and Daniel Boniche kneel at the altar in their prayer room.*

I spend a morning with Gloria Saballos and her husband, Daniel Boniche, at their church in Managua. They tell me about reaching out to the poor neighborhood to the south of the church in the past five years, and now it has less alcoholism, abuse, and danger.

A sanctuary banner displays the church mission for 2010: "We speak, we walk, and we believe, because the eyes of the Lord are over us."

Sundays, five hundred people worship here. Monday through Friday, movable panels are pulled out, and the church becomes a school for three hundred.

A few years ago, when the school outgrew the church, the congregation added adjacent classroom space. Gloria, an architect as well as a teacher-trainer, designed both the balconies and the adjacent classrooms. As noon nears, Gloria invites me to their home. "I want to show you my special place," she says, her voice warm with love.

"Ah, an architect-designer," I think. "Of course—she loves her home."

We enter, but she provides no house tour. She takes me directly to the second floor, up rough cement steps, past thinly painted walls, through an open-air walkway, to a pair of paneled doors.

She stops, hand on the door, turns back to me, and says, "I used to climb a ladder and lie on the roof to be alone with God. Slowly, as God provided and allowed, we have made this place."

She opens the double doors to her family's prayer room: tiled floors, elegant wood-patterned walls, graceful windows, and an altar—a wooden stand with a container of papers. She shows me the papers—pages of church needs dotted with Post-it notes recording God's answers, other papers with penciled plans.

Here they meet for family prayer, sometimes kneeling, sometimes sitting. Here when Gloria is seeking an answer to prayer alone, she lies prone before the altar. Here their daughter Irene, thirteen, dances praise to God.

I realize later, as we tour the remaining rooms, it is by far the most beautiful and spacious room in their home—a space that energizes their believing, speaking, and walking under the gaze of their Lord.

In a house that is, by North American standards, tiny, a room reserved for prayer alone is a very special place indeed.

Both the church and the school take advantage of many of the Nehemiah Center's training programs, including the Christian-school Excelencia materials described in more detail in Chapter 7. Within the church, there is growing tolerance for differing economic and educational levels and styles of worship that come from the different barrios. "Depending on their neighborhood, some jump and shout; others are more quiet and reflective," said Gloria.

Besides her work as an architect, Gloria serves as a trainer for the Nicaraguan association of Christian schools. Gloria also works in the local school run by the church she and Daniel pastor, equipping the teachers with better classroom practices and helping them to integrate the Bible into their teaching. In the church, Gloria trains Sunday school teachers and takes on many other pastoral duties as well, including preaching. She also has used her architectural skills to revise her church's building so that it can be used weekdays as a school.

"From the beginning, God told me not to separate things," said Gloria. "In the Nehemiah Center training in worldview, we learned to see through God's eyes and integrate all things. Through God's strength, I integrate architecture, school, and pastoral work. We were a small church with a little piece of land, and the parents wanted a safe place for their kids because the public school was dangerous with gangs. We looked at how the church could do that. And here comes [my background in] architecture to help."

As pastor, Daniel often preaches on Sunday mornings and Tuesday evenings, but he sometimes steps back, too, encouraging both women and men to preach and develop their skills.

As director of the Nehemiah Center, Daniel continues to encourage new leadership and improve relations.

"I always think God does marvelous things through people. I have to learn how to trust in what God does through different persons," said Daniel. "The Nehemiah Center has committed people who know about God's teaching. This makes the work easy, not that it is small, but it is easier when people have a conscious desire to serve God to the limit of the capacity in them and the desire to share what is being done. [As a result,] there is a support team with more experience and that helps us direct the Nehemiah Center.

"Within God's plan, there is a special place for the church," Daniel continued. "Every time I read the Bible and hear a Christian preacher, I know God always has a plan to expand his kingdom through the church. And the Nehemiah Center is special in teaching Christians how to expand the kingdom and mobilize all areas of the church."

Mobilizing all areas of the church, as Daniel said, is important, but this can only happen when churches are healthy. Just as healthy marriages lead to stronger and more effective pastors, so healthy churches lead to congregations that are more willing and able to work in their communities. However, these steps are only a start. From these beginnings, much more transformational work can develop.

FROM CAROL'S JOURNAL
## On Visions

It's June 2009 and the book interviews have just begun. Seated in a corner conference room of the Nehemiah Center, I listen to Daniel Boniche tell me about his vision.

Having completed two different master's programs in engineering, Daniel was working as a government engineer. He considered pastoring very difficult work and had no interest in becoming a pastor. However, his church pastor had confidence in Daniel, often assigned him congregational volunteer roles, and left him in charge when called out of town. Daniel obediently complied.

One Sunday morning on a beach with his family before morning worship, Daniel had prayed, 'Lord, whatever you want from me, I will do it.' Then during the service, something strange happened.

'While I was praying, I saw what was like a treasure chest in the air. As a Baptist, I did not expect this. I said, 'This isn't biblical.' But what I was seeing was reality. I saw this treasure chest come into the church building. I waited to see where it would go. And I was surprised that after moving through the church, the chest came into my hands. My question was, 'What in the world does God want of me?'

'I spent the whole day and night asking God, 'What does this mean?''

Driving his yellow jeep to work Monday morning, he continued to ask. And he heard God's voice, audible and clear. God said, 'My church is my special treasure. Take care of it.'

Daniel's initial interpretation: continue volunteering for his jobs as a deacon with children, youth, and elderly, but give even more of himself to these jobs.

Three months later, the church pastor announced he was running for political office, would leave his role as pastor, and asked Daniel and Gloria to meet him. Then he told them the congregation was asking that Daniel replace him as pastor.

'I had already told the Lord I would do whatever he wanted. So I said yes.' And for twelve years, Daniel and Gloria have led this congregation.

As I listen to Daniel, I keep my face and body composed, but questions clamor: An audible voice? I've never heard God's audible voice. Is he embroidering his story for dramatic effect? Did he imagine it?

In my later conversation with Joel Huyser, one of the Nehemiah Center's founders, I ask for his wisdom. 'Do you really think he saw a vision and heard an audible voice?' I ask. 'And should I include it in the book? I'm not sure this will be credible to some of our North American readers.'

Joel tells me he thinks it is very similar to a North American saying, 'I had a thought.' Hmm. It doesn't seem that similar to me. This question sits silent, unanswered in me for eighteen months.

And then back in Pella after a 2011 visit to Nicaragua with my church team, I listen to my pastor, Gary Hanson, describe going for his regular walk now that he has returned home.

*(continued on next page)*

FROM CAROL'S JOURNAL
## *On Visions (continued)*

Many evenings he has walked by a house with a for-sale sign in the front yard. And many evenings he has dreamed of it as a wonderful larger space for his young family.

Earlier, while part of the church team in Nicaragua, he visited Caroray at the church where she was being tutored. Gary and his family have corresponded with and sponsored Caroray for four years, under a Compassion International program. Caroray lives in a congested neighborhood on the edge of the Managua city dump where many residents scrape together a living by scavenging recently discarded garbage for recyclables. Gary was deeply aware when he waved goodbye to her that although he could leave, she was staying in this neighborhood that Compassion International had deemed too dangerous for him to visit her at home.

The first evening back from Nicaragua, he again daydreamed of owning the larger home as he walked by. It would be good to have more space. Then he chuckled as a new thought flashed. "Seriously!? How much do you think you need, Gary?" As he smiled, he knew he didn't need a larger home. Changed by meeting Caroray, he recognized the materialism in his heart. "It was a humbling experience," he says.

Then he hesitates. "I don't think I'm prone to hear a voice from God, and I'm not sure God uses language like 'Seriously?!' but . . ." He stops short of identifying his thought as the voice of God.

As I listen to my pastor, I remember reading about cultural conditioning of Christians in different countries. Against a background of the supernaturalism of indigenous Central American religions, Nicaraguan Christians are likely to interpret experiences as visions and God's voice. Conditioned by individualistic materialism, North Americans are likely to interpret them as personal thoughts.

And I flash back to my earlier conversations with Daniel and Joel. At last I have a glimmer of an answer to my long-buried question.

A vision or imagination? The voice of God or a thought? In the end, it may not matter. In the final analysis, the two may be one.

But this, I think is crucial: a soft heart, open to divine love and leading, no matter what I am conditioned to name it.

Managua as seen from Parque Histórico Nacional Loma de Tiscapa, a national park overlooking the city

# 07

## Not Our Land

*It is hard to hear about biblical worldview and not fall in love with it.*

*-REYNA CHAVARRÍA, NICARAGUAN TEACHER IN ESTELI*

When Daniel Aragón and Darling Hüeck bought land in December 1999 in Cedro Galan, an area just south of Managua, the couple looked forward eagerly—albeit patiently—to building a home. They invited friends to a dedication ceremony for their future home. "We will let the Lord build the house when he is ready," they said.

As they cleaned that property on weekends, they met their neighbors. To their shock, they discovered the children—even teenagers—could not read. Many children in this *comarca* of five thousand had never attended school. That disturbed them.

So, Daniel and Darling started teaching Sunday school under the trees. That Sunday school soon became a Bible club—which also included a meal. Under those same trees, it also became a church, with Daniel as its pastor. In time, the husband-wife team also found themselves starting daily primary school classes on the porches of three neighborhood homes.

Earlier in 1999, Daniel had been recommended as a Spanish tutor to Eric and Marilyn Loftsgard, newly arrived in Nicaragua, "He came to tutor us with Darling, and sometimes with his whole family," said Eric. That connection became an important one for both couples. They soon discovered a mutual Christianity, shared interests, and became friends. Daniel and Darling shared their passion to educate the children of Cedro Galan with the Loftsgards.

Simultaneously, Missionary Ventures, with whom Eric worked, had a North American team slated to build a school near the Managua city dump. "But that project was showing all sorts of red flags," said Eric. "In fact, that was a failure. So, here we were with a team coming, and no school for them to build! The problem was we had started doling out money and goods where there was not a ministry already in progress."

Not wanting to make the same mistake, Eric approached Daniel and Darling with a proposal. If they would donate land for the school, he had a team that would help build one. The couple consented.

Within a year after their dedication ceremony for their future home, Daniel and Darling opened a school—not a home—on that land.

## In and Out of War

*Darling   Hüeck   and   Daniel Aragón*

Daniel, a large black-haired man with a deep voice and a penchant for both philosophy and flowery descriptions, met his future wife while they both were in high school. Daniel and Darling, a petite Nicaraguan redhead with German ancestry, got to know each other in the Baptist church where they both committed their lives to God. Just after graduating, they married.

Daniel went on to study at the university, which, in the mid-1970s, was full of student protests against the repressive Somoza regime in which being caught with a Marxist book was grounds for execution. Daniel asked his church for answers to his questions about social justice. Stay out of such issues, he was told. They belonged to the world. But he wouldn't, couldn't. "When I met Marxism, I found a philosophical answer to my questions, 'Why is there injustice?' and 'Why is there war?'"

Convinced that Marxism defined the good side and as a Christian he should be on that side, he joined the Sandinistas in 1978, a decision Darling supported, proud of his action to improve their country. Daniel climbed through the ranks as an intelligence officer. Though he didn't go to church, he still considered himself a Christian.

By 1983, the Sandinistas had taken control of the country, but counter-revolutionary groups (Contras) were growing. In his work as a Sandinista intelligence officer, Daniel secretly filmed a priest believed to be plotting to set off a bomb with the intent of blaming the Sandinistas for the resulting deaths. His discovery of that plot became a public scandal and international news.

For Daniel, this event was the catalyst that precipitated his loss of faith in God.

Dark years followed for the country and for the couple. For Nicaragua, the decade of the 1980s was filled with chaos, poverty, instability, and violence. For Daniel and Darling, those were years of drugs, alcohol, marital infidelity, failed businesses, and disillusionment with the Sandinista government.

Daniel watched the changing values of some leaders in the Sandinista army—leaders who were enjoying luxuries unthinkable to others in the country suffering at that time under a U.S. trade embargo. Smoking Marlboros and owning expensive homes full of video recorders, colored televisions, and other luxuries were definitely not practices of the equality espoused by Marxism.

When Daniel spoke out against these practices, the Sandinista party expelled him and put him in jail for a month. His troubles continued upon his release: Darling told him she wanted out of their marriage. "I was so tired of him being indifferent to me, of his cheating, of his abandonment," said Darling. "He was being a jerk. He even wanted to bring his ladies to our house."

Instead of dealing with the situation, Daniel fled, ultimately landing in San Bernardino, California, in October 1989. Darling did not press for a divorce, and briefly joined him, along with their daughter. She didn't like living in the United States, however; so when Violeta Barrios de Chamorro won the Nicaraguan presidency in 1990, ending the Sandinista rule, the couple returned to Nicaragua.

Their troubled life did not improve. After Daniel's father died in 1991 and left him homes and vehicles, Daniel started using drugs. Darling joined him. For at least two years, the couple

## Cutting the Bonds of Witchcraft

One of the religious influences in Nicaragua is witchcraft. Daniel Aragón and Darling Hüeck believe their household was at one time under its influence.

In the mid-1990s, Daniel bought drugs from Sonya, a Miskito woman who was a medium. One day, Sonya told him that someone was practicing witchcraft on him. "I didn't believe her, of course. I didn't believe in those things," said Daniel. Sonya told him that he should search his house and garden. Skeptical, Daniel and Darling did so.

"We found crushed crystals tied with human hair, in blue bags," said Daniel. "In the garden, I saw things that if I hadn't seen them, I would not have believed them. There were these weird plants. A maid had planted them there. The roots of these plants were huge like ginger roots, and the roots were in the shape of animals, scorpions, and spiders—very defined."

When they reported back to the Miskito woman, she claimed God had told her of their problem, and she gave them special substances to put in their house, special water to shower in, and told them that in six months, when their fortune changed, they should pay her $1,000.

Daniel and Darling took the shower, but then Daniel started meditating. "And I said, this is not a characteristic of God. Maybe God told a message to this woman for me, but the actions are not from God."

Still, Daniel returned to Sonya to buy drugs. But when he returned home, he prayed. "I asked him to forgive me. I said 'God, I can't leave this, but you are powerful to liberate me from this. When you believe I am prepared, take me out of this. I will wait on you.' "

Five days later, Daniel and Darling went to church and reconciled with the Lord in front of everyone. "And then we went back home and destroyed everything we had—the cocaine, burned all the porn tapes, the books I read."

were on- and off-again drug users.

Finally, after multiple interventions by Christian friends, they confessed to God and got rid of the drugs for good in April 1997.

Together, they started attending church, where their paths again crossed with friends from their Sandinista years, Daniel Boniche and Gloria Saballos. "His long-haired hippie friend was now a pastor!" said Daniel Boniche. Over the next year, he discipled Daniel and Darling, who practically lived with the pastoral couple, all the while asking questions and learning from them as role models. "Daniel [Aragón] has a very philosophical mind and would ask me incredibly philosophical questions," said Daniel Boniche. "The Lord gave me the grace to respond appropriately."

At this time in their lives, Daniel and Darling had closed two businesses and had no income. So, this high-energy couple became busy volunteers, at first teaching children from Boniche's church on Saturdays. They started training others to teach, and the number of children grew exponentially. Daniel started writing a manual for the teachers.

For income, Daniel taught a mathematics class and also began teaching Spanish to missionaries, including the Loftsgards.

As his friendship with Eric Loftsgard grew, Daniel began hearing about the Nehemiah Center and biblical worldview—a philosophy to replace his Marxism. "For me it was like I was reborn—similar to a baptism of the Holy Spirit," said Daniel. "It touched all of me . . . There was a transformation in all of me. In my whole body.

"I think the Holy Spirit anointed me to a specific work, a task I was going to do. The task of education."

Daniel shared what he was learning with Darling. "I had a tendency just to see the spiritual side, the legalistic side," said Darling. "I would have to go every day to church. If I didn't go, I would feel very condemned by God." Darling listened to Daniel, read books, attended seminars, and saw the importance of creation. "It was like coverings fell from my eyes."

As they received training under the Nehemiah Center, Daniel and Darling began training others that everything belonged to God and they were to be his hands in it. Some years later they both also began working on master's degrees in education.

They prepared themselves to devote their lives to sharing biblical worldview through Christian education—starting with the school they launched on three front porches, now Mount Hermon Christian School.

## Mount Hermon School

Just ten years ago, Nery Martínez could not read. It wasn't that she didn't want to learn; she wanted to learn desperately. But her mom, a single mother of five who worked as a maid cleaning other people's houses, couldn't afford to send Nery and her siblings to school. Though public school

Nery Martinez

was considered free, the family couldn't afford the uniforms, the books, and other materials they would need.

It wasn't until she was thirteen that Nery finally started school. Eager to read, she learned quickly and finished six years of primary school in four years. At twenty-one, she finished her secondary education at Mount Hermon Christian School.

Now, at twenty-three, Nery teaches third grade in that same school and is in her third year of study at the university. She dreams both of getting married and of getting more education, perhaps becoming a university teacher or psychologist. Without school, she knows exactly what her life would be like. "I would be a stay-at-home mother with children already. I wouldn't be in the university at all. I wouldn't be able to read."

Opening doors for people like Nery is exactly what Daniel and Darling had in mind when they opened the doors of *Colegio Cristiano Monte Hermón* (Mount Hermon Christian School). That first year, forty-six students in grades one through three walked through its doors. That same year, the school achieved an unusual feat for a Nicaraguan school: all forty-six students completed the school year.

Darling commuted thirty kilometers daily from Rubenia, a barrio on the eastern side of Managua, to Cedro Galan to teach as a volunteer; she received no salary. The second year, grades four through six were added as afternoon classes. Darling was still commuting, directing the school and teaching by day while teaching adult education classes in the same building by night. In March of the second year, Daniel and Darling moved to the comarca, into a home that Missionary Ventures had helped to build on the property the couple had given up for the school. That home also immediately became home to some of the teachers. Daniel and Darling's children shared their small bedrooms with teachers whom their parents welcomed into their home.

Darling hadn't been at the school very long before she and other staff members realized that hungry children could not learn. So, they started feeding the children, using soy as a staple because soybeans were cheap.

Gradually, they saw real changes in the students. Darling recalled asking some of her students at the beginning of the year what they wanted to be when they grew up. Their responses were typical of their situation in society: a gardener, pastor, or cook. Darling told them that God might have other ideas for them. At the end of the year, she asked the question again. "They answered a lawyer, or policeman, or teacher. Their minds had changed," Darling said.

"The ones I gave classes to the first year are now out of high school, and they are studying in the university. They changed the way they looked at the world. That is the best gift God gives us—after Jesus Christ—this satisfaction."

In 2011, a decade after opening its doors, Mount Hermon school had 142 primary school

## NCA: An Evolving Vision for Future Nicaraguan Leaders

*Liam Starkenburg*

Asked his vision for the Nicaragua Christian Academy (NCA), Director Liam Starkenburg stopped multitasking at his office keyboard, and responded, "How long do you have? I've given entire presentations on this."

Liam came to this U.S.-accredited, preschool-through-secondary Christian school in Managua as its computer science instructor in 2000 and has been director of NCA for six years.

Asked for the short version, he immediately and passionately responded, "That NCA graduates will one day be leaders who make a difference in Nicaragua—in government, education, business, and beyond—in a way that honors God."

He explained that this is a dramatically counter-cultural vision for Nicaraguan youth. In a 2007 survey, many were asked, "If you could leave Nicaragua—never to return—would you?" For eighty-four percent, the answer was yes—even if they could never come home again.

"They have no hope for the future of their country," Liam said.

All NCA graduating students are asked to share their plans in senior presentations, held a month before they graduate. Although some Nicaraguan students plan to study abroad, they consistently describe goals of working for the transformation of Nicaragua. NCA tracks its graduates, and they are living out those plans.

When NCA was launched in 1991, it was a school only for the English-speaking children of North American missionaries. Its founders soon had requests from upper-middle-class Nicaraguans who could afford the tuition for their children to attend, and they agreed.

In 2002, as enrollment surpassed 250, the school was reaching maximum capacity. Its governing board wrestled with an ongoing vision. Longtime board member Eric Loftsgard remembered, "We didn't want to make a self-serving choice. We wanted to base our decision on principle and a spirit of service." In its exploration, the board discovered an educational gap. Neighborhood schools in Nicaraguan churches educated very low-income children, who might not otherwise learn to read. NCA served missionary children and more affluent Nicaraguans. However, lower-middle-class Nicaraguans valued a good education, and they could not afford NCA tuition rates.

A new vision evolved: create a lower-cost, Spanish-speaking school for these families. Out of this new vision, NCA Nejapa was born on land bordering the Nehemiah Center. It opened in 2005 with fifty-three students. By 2011, it had 326 students in preschool through secondary school; its enrollment had surpassed NCA's by twenty-eight students. "We were blown away when we saw how fast it grew," said Eric.

In the face of that amazing growth, the governing board now has an expanded vision—to replicate an NCA Nejapa in each of the five major cities of Nicaragua.

students with an average class size of less than twenty-four students. Another fifty-four children were in the secondary grades with an average class size of eleven students. It also had a preschool.

Ninety percent of the students at Mount Hermon school pay nothing for their education. The others pay the equivalent of a dollar or two a month. The rest of the school's monthly $4,300 budget is funded by the Mount Hermon church that oversees the school, and by donors and sponsors of students, primarily from North America.

*Mount Hermon school primary classroom*

Teacher salaries average $120 per month—roughly $80 a month less than in public schools. Janitorial duties are rotated among school families. "We think our students receive a blessing when they are able to pay something. The students and their parents are in charge of cleaning their school. That is a way of them paying something," said Elsa Madrigal, who has been Mount Hermon principal for five years.

Most of its teachers completed a three-year training program that they entered either in ninth grade or after eleventh grade. Some, like Elsa, completed college education while they were teaching.

Mount Hermon is a government-accredited school. In primary grades, students learn reading, writing, math, geography, Nicaraguan history, and Central American history. In secondary school, physics, chemistry, world history, geography, and physical education are part of the course work.

Students in grades three through eleven also learn computer skills. Although the school owns seventeen computers, students only use ten at a time because that's the maximum the electrical system can handle. There is no Internet access.

Students do not have textbooks. Teachers use teacher's editions of the approved textbooks, and stay current on changes to those textbooks and the curriculum by going online at Internet cafes. Students attend class from 7 a.m. until noon. Two days each week, thirty-six percent of the primary students receive a noon meal and additional tutoring under a Compassion International program. At noon, high school students head to the fields to work.

FROM CAROL'S JOURNAL
### *Cooking Tortillas*

Karla Vanessa, a thirty-year-old mother of two, spends eight or nine hours per day working at her Managua streetside tortilla stand.

She fires up her wood-burning stove at 5 a.m., and closes up shop at 6 p.m., taking breaks during the slow-traffic periods mid-morning and mid-afternoon.

On an average day she sells two hundred to three hundred corn tortillas for one córdoba (about five cents) each. The corn flour for each one costs her half that.

She and a business partner alternate cooking with hand-shaping the tortillas so each of them gets a break from the harder and hotter work at the stove. They split the profits.

I ask how she spends her half, and she replies, 'For my children to go to school.' It pays for uniforms, shoes, backpacks, notebooks, and pencils.

*Making tortillas*

During harvest season, students even as young as six or eight drop out of school to help their families harvest corn and beans. If they do return after harvest, they often don't ask for the help they need to catch up. Frequently, Mount Hermon teachers must visit students at home, encouraging them to return to class, and offering to help them catch up.

## Nicaraguan Government Schools

Until the Sandinista literacy campaign in 1980, illiteracy in Nicaragua hovered close to fifty percent. Even today, education opportunities are limited for many. Public schools in the country are crowded, poorly financed, and often in disrepair. Until recently, attendance was required only through sixth grade. Now, although attendance is officially free and compulsory through eleventh grade, the law is not enforced, and many children do not attend school. The cost to transport children to the schools, combined with the cost of uniforms, shoes, and materials, puts education out of reach for many.

It isn't just the costs that discourage attendance. There is a shortage of school buildings, teachers, desks, and textbooks. In some classes, particularly in the lower grades, there are a hundred students per classroom. In rural areas, students may need to walk five or ten kilometers to school, and there may be just one teacher for all six grades. Sometimes teachers live far away and spend a good part of Monday and Friday traveling; sometimes they don't show up at all. Even when teachers and students are in the classroom, the education still falls short. Students often just copy and regurgitate what the teacher writes on the blackboard. Violence is often a concern.

Officially, twenty percent of the population is illiterate, but that rate surpasses forty percent among the poorer people in the country. About half of the students do not pass grade four. Only about thirty percent finish high school, and only eight percent get a college degree.[1]

Because of these conditions in government schools, over the years evangelical churches have started Christian schools. Many of these churches were motivated by the inability of neighborhood children to read and write and their failure to attend school. Churches frequently held classes in the church building with Sunday school teachers as volunteer teachers.

Whether these Christian schools were significantly better than the public schools is debatable. Probably some were, and some weren't. In many of these schools the teachers weren't trained, not in pedagogy and certainly not in a philosophy of Christian education. Though the intentions were good, the educational quality was erratic. In addition, the schools were isolated; no one even had a clue how many of these private schools existed in the country.

## Rise of the Christian School System

By 2000, Christian teachers in Managua were beginning to get together in workshops sponsored by Missionary Ventures to share information at educational roundtables. Daniel Aragón and Darling Hüeck were key trainers. Later, as the Nehemiah Center's Ezra education staff person, Daniel also traveled to other regions of Nicaragua, both to train teachers and to train teachers who would train other teachers. Worldwide Christian Schools–U.S. and Christian Schools International helped fund his work.

*Mount Hermon high school classroom*

Locating isolated Christian schools across the country proved difficult, however, until one principal produced a list of forty Christian schools. "One school took us to another school, and in three years, we had a list of 167," said Daniel. "Nobody had a list before; no one knew how many schools there were. These schools were from different denominations—Assembly of God, Baptist,

---

[1]"Service and Learning Teams: Pre-field Information Guide, 2010-2011," The Nehemiah Center.

Central American, Church of God—all different denominations."

Emerging was a growing realization of the need for collaboration among these isolated Christian schools. "In 2004, the association of schools wanted to get organized because of this movement. It was born within them, not from us," said Daniel. "ACECEN (*Asociación de Centros Educativos Cristianas Evangélicas de Nicaragua*) was born with twenty-three schools."

Again, the path was difficult at first. Different people had different visions; one board member stole from the organization. But by 2007, sixty schools were part of the association. Key people from many regions came monthly to the Nehemiah Center for training, then went home and trained others. As of 2009, membership had grown to 123 schools.

## Tesoros de Dios Serves Children with Disabilities

In Nicaraguan culture, children with disabilities are sometimes hidden at home, a shame invisible to surrounding community. It is not unusual for their fathers to take no interest in them, reject them, and even desert the entire family.

In 2011, *Tesoros de Dios* (God's Treasures) served about eighty-five Managua-area children with physical and mental disabilities, many of them children of single mothers in dire need and grateful for the educational support.

Lilliam, mother of an eleven-year-old son with autism, said, for example, "I give thanks to God above all because Tesoros de Dios has given me the help and support I have needed with my son. I am also thankful for all the teachers because they have had all the patience in the world to work with my son, and they have taught him everything he knows today. I eternally say 'thank you.'"

Tesoros de Dios opened in 2004 as a farm-based pilot project for horse therapy for two disabled children, and grew rapidly. In 2005, Ohio Pastor Jim Wilson, whose son Bradley had disabilities, saw the program in action, returned to Ohio, and raised funding for a building.

In 2006, Michelle Adams, former teacher of special education at Nicaragua Christian Academy, joined the staff and shortly after became director. Tesoros de Dios has a staff of ten Nicaraguans-teachers, physical therapists, and other support staff. Jeannie Huyser, wife of Nehemiah Center co-founder Joel Huyser, is a volunteer member of the staff.

Several of its current and former students are now mainstreamed into area schools, an accomplishment they could not have achieved without this program. All services are free of charge, and funding is provided through donations, primarily from the United States. Tesoros de Dios operates under *Fundación El Samaritano* (Samaritan Foundation), a Nicaraguan nonprofit organization.

This school is a vision-become-reality for Michelle. "In my first years in Nicaragua, I had a dream of starting a special education school because of seeing rough conditions in an orphanage for kids with disabilities."

Michelle observed that in recent years she has noticed more Nicaraguan people and agencies interested in serving children with special needs.

Starting in 2007, USAID funded a program in private schools that taught a new teaching method. This U.S. organization, the economic development arm of the U.S. Secretary of State, already had been funneling money to improve public education.

The program, called *Excelencia* (Excellence), was intended to replace the commonly used rote memorization learning methods with a more interactive, participatory learning style. At the same time, the program encouraged parent and community involvement.

USAID chose the Nehemiah Center as its local partner. The Nehemiah Center used ACECEN as the organization to implement it.  Wanting the program to reflect its Christian identity, coordinators named the program *Ester* (Esther) *Excelencia,* after an Old Testament Israelite who had saved her nation from destruction. Darling Hüeck became director while her husband Daniel continued his work on the Ezra staff for the Nehemiah Center.

ACECEN proved worthy of the assignment.  Excelencia programs and their predecessors had been in government schools for fifteen years.  But after just two years, student test scores in Christian schools with Ester Excelencia programs surpassed scores from government schools with the Excelencia programs. In 2009, the eighteen-month Excelencia program ended. Evaluators have told ACECEN that its program was very successful, and it is in contention for additional funding should programming be resumed. However, as of 2011, USAID still had its education program in Nicaragua on hold.  ACECEN has been able to continue the teacher-training program on a reduced level thanks to a partnership with EduDeo Ministries (formerly Worldwide Christian Schools-Canada).

## Discovering the 'Christian' in Christian Schools

In 1997, Reyna Chavarría took a fifty percent pay cut and joined the staff at Emaus school, the first-ever Christian school in Esteli, a city a couple hours' drive north of Managua.

"We were very joyful when we started, but we weren't very clear about what a Christian school was," Reyna remembered. She knew it was not the same as Sunday school, not just about Bible classes, but was uncertain where to start with her students.

A 2001 education conference at the Nehemiah Center provided some answers, and she still has those training documents—and uses them regularly. "At that first training we found out what we were supposed to be doing in Christian education," she said. "Before that, we had the desire, but no know-how."

She learned about the cultural mandate, the great commission, and the great commandment. And she learned principles such as showing respect for students as images of God, servant leadership, participatory learning, the need to define vision and mission, and the use of materials from students' daily lives as teaching tools.

As mentioned earlier, Nicaraguan teaching traditionally regards students as empty con-

## The Importance of Clarifying Roles

One crucial catalyst in Nicaraguan education who trained and inspired teacher Reyna Chavarría and others was North American John Van Dyk, formerly a professor of educational philosophy at Dordt College in Sioux Center, Iowa. Upon his retirement, he joined Alta Vista, a Seattle-based organization devoted to improving Christian education.

A lifelong, passionate proponent of Christian philosophy, John had considerable international teaching experience before he trained Nicaraguan teachers. His areas of special expertise include worldview, the relation between worldview and philosophy of education, implementing philosophy of education, topics in educational leadership, cooperative learning strategies, lesson-planning, and more.

His teaching helped many Christian teachers like Reyna who needed to hear his teaching that the roles of each person need to be clear. "As vice-principal I was doing the teaching, administration, bathroom cleaning, speaking to the community," said Reyna. "When everyone does everything, it is like trying to hit a piñata blindfolded. On the trip back from Managua, I asked the principal what my focus was going to be."

Reyna paused, her mouth turned up and a few smile lines appeared around her clear eyes. "She said, 'The same as before—everything!'" Then they worked together to define their focus and roles.

*Reyna Chavarría makes a point.*

tainers to be filled with information and relies heavily on rote memorization. At the Nehemiah Center and through the Excelencia program, Reyna learned to use a more interactive method—using familiar items such as students' own names to teach the alphabet and simulating *pulperia* (in-home shops) purchases to teach numbers. She saw how students learned these basics in a fraction of the time that they had required before.

Similarly, Reyna—who is now president of ACECEN—has learned how getting the parents involved can improve education. At Emaus, for example, parent projects have funded equipment such as a tape recorder and DVD player. Parents also assist with holiday activities.

Critical to the success of schools like Emaus is the passion these Christian teachers have for their work—most could make higher salaries in the public schools. Staff members work in Christian schools because they believe it is their calling, so, they spend extra time after school to do research at Internet cafes, make personal visits to students' homes, prepare lunches for the students, and do whatever is necessary to ensure that students are successful.

Reyna's particular passion has been to empower others. "Now, when some schools ask me to provide training or do something for them, I say, 'You have the person or the resources right in your own school to do that!' Or sometimes I say, 'I will help you, but YOU will do it.' "

*Standing in the exterior hallway, Reyna Chavarria shows a visitor the Emaus school grounds.*

## FROM CAROL'S JOURNAL
### *Reaching into Unexpected Places*

As teacher Iveth Gauffreau talks with Daniel, Darling, and me, she opens a notebook that lists in neat columns the places she has taught evening classes, the members of each class, their addresses, and telephone numbers. Daniel is startled to see the denomination of two congregations on her list—*Iglesia Apostolica* (Apostolic Church).

This denomination is radically conservative, he explains to me. Women wear head coverings, no makeup, and no jewelry. "How do you dress?" he asks Iveth.

"As I am now," she answers. She smiles, attractively made up with both mascara and lipstick. "If I get stuck, I'll call you to help me!

"The people from the Apostolica churches want to meet both of you," she tells the couple. "So do my mother and grandmother."

"The honor and glory be to God," Darling responds.

"You go places I couldn't," Daniel tells Iveth, shaking his head. "By myself I would never be accepted in an Apostolica church."

Daniel is surprised by what he is hearing. So am I.

*Darling Hüeck says farewell to the Colegio Emaus school principal after a visit to the school.*

Another teacher who benefited from the Ester Excelencia program is Iveth Gauffreau, a vibrant and passionate teacher from Chinandega. In 2007, like Reyna, Iveth became an Ester Excelencia trainer for eleven schools in her area.

Just two years earlier, she had attended her first Christian teacher training. What she heard surprised her. "I expected them to talk to me about the Bible, of course, but after that, the trainings kept going. I found out this was a way to see the world as God sees it." She had seen the world and the church as separated, a job as just a necessity to earn money, and community involvement as sinful. "But, *gracias a Dios* (thanks to God), my mind was opened. I learned about the cultural mandate, servant leadership, and holistic service."

She completed all three levels of worldview training offered by the Nehemiah Center, then worked alongside Daniel and Darling as a trainer for a year.

Iveth has since organized her own training sessions, expanding into area churches as well as schools. She wasn't always welcomed. "My church thought I was far too liberal. My pastor said he didn't know if I was Assembly of God anymore—I was always at the Nehemiah Center. But now he is cured of that." He saw that the Nehemiah Center did not steal her from her congregation or denomination, but sent her back to teach and to preach. "With the help of the Holy Spirit, he has been opening his mind."

She also introduced churches to HIV/AIDS awareness training and to Buen Trato. "They say they want more . . . more . . . I also told them sex is blessed by God in the sanctity of marriage—many of them saw it as vulgar and sinful."

Through Iveth, the multiplication blessing continues.

Traveling back to Managua from their meeting with Iveth, Daniel and Darling rejoiced in the transformation taking place, and they reminisced about the unpredictable twists in their married life. They remembered the hardships but looked back with joy at the transformations they witnessed and fostered.

In addition to donating land to build that school in Cedro Galan, they have given away and sold other parcels to expand the school, to build a sanctuary for Mount Hermon church, and to pay for their daughter's flight to the United States to attend college. They currently own no land, and continue living in the home adjacent to the church and school.

Daniel glanced at Darling and asked, "I wonder what we would do if we ever own land again."

Without a moment's pause, Darling responded, "We'd probably give it to the church!"

They both laughed uproariously.

Plantain tree

# 08

## From Dirt Eaters to Artisans

*We see ourselves as equals, not bigger or smaller.*

-EL OJOCHE RESIDENT AT COMMUNITY MEETING, JANUARY 2010

In 2000, garbage, disagreement, disease, malnutrition, and death consumed the tiny village of El Ojoche, in northeast Nicaragua.

"Because we work with clay, our clothes were always dirty," recalled one village resident. "People called us pigs, and wouldn't eat food from our houses." Derisively, the villagers were known as iguana-eaters—catching, selling, and eating the lizards as only the very poor would do. Parents of adolescents from neighboring villages refused to allow their youth to date El Ojoche residents.

Even within the village there was division: a streambed divided El Ojoche into two parts, and residents on one side of the streambed considered themselves superior to the other side. Catholics and Protestants were also sharply divided.

That streambed provided the community with water when the rainy season began in May, but by the end of October when the rains stopped, the river became a trickle, then dried up completely. The nearest spring was a two-hour walk away.

This village of eighty-five families hadn't always been like this. When it was settled around 1900, the area was a lush, fertile clay belt. Over the years the forest was cut down, and gradually the micro-climate changed. It became a scorching-hot, dusty area with sparse rainfall. Except for the clay, the community might long ago have been abandoned. Residents used the clay for bricks and roofing tiles to build their homes, and sold some for extra income. Working with the clay was hot, dirty work, and the clay worked its

*El Ojoche potter with her wares*

way under their skin—resulting in their dirty appearance and reputation.

Families grew corn, beans, and sorghum on tiny clay-soil plots to feed their families. Typically, families only ate tortillas, rice, and beans—three times a day, 365 days a year.

Though the town's stream provided water during the rainy season, too frequently village children died from its contaminated water. During the dry season, they were often hungry and thirsty. Men left their families to find temporary employment elsewhere. The local government had given up on El Ojoche, abandoning it to whatever fate developed for it. It was considered one of the poorest communities of the province, the least organized, and having the least potential.

In 2002, a couple of strangers began showing up regularly from nearby Somotillo. El Ojoche people heard about possibilities for training and education—training that offered the possibility of a better future, if they were willing to participate and work for it. These strangers told the villagers they would need to organize, work together, plan, and make decisions about their wants and needs.

Some of the villagers were skeptical. Training? They didn't need training. They needed money and supplies—and food and water during the dry season. This program didn't offer that, they learned. Only training. One local pastor remembered, "When Herberth first came, I was not happy with the program. We were always accepting training and nothing was happening."

Even so, Herberth Reyes, one of the visitors to El Ojoche, saw potential. He saw possibilities even if not all the residents could see it themselves.

"We had already visited several other communities who did not meet our program requirements," said Herberth. "In El Ojoche, there was some opposition, but we also found people interested in working for change, and we decided to start with El Ojoche."

## 'Touch me. Change me.'

Herberth, a lean forty-one-year-old with a slight rounding to his shoulders and spine that gives him an ongoing look of deference on every occasion, had lived through dramatic changes of his own.

Bumping along the road from Somotillo to El Ojoche in January 2010 in a small, red car on loan for the day, Herberth told his story as Nathan Sandahl of Food for the Hungry drove and translated. At that time, Herberth was in his tenth year as a community health trainer for Community Health Evangelism (CHE), a program that aims to train local volunteers to improve spiritual, physical, emotional, and social health.

However, before 2001, Herberth said, his life was "completely disorganized."

"My parents and grandparents taught me a little about God, but in Spain I stopped believing he existed." Sent to Spain for training as a Sandinista youth coordinator, he worshipped in empty churches, was mocked when he used the phrase *Gracias a Dios* (thanks to God) in conversation, and was shocked to see thinly clad beggars shivering in the streets, ignored by Christians. "In a

*Herberth Reyes (left) with El Ojoche resident*

country with riches and wealth, no one helped them. At that point, I said, 'Not a single person is going to convince me God exists. It has all been deception.'"

As a soldier, he had begun using alcohol and drugs, and those addictions continued; as a result, he mistreated his family. An acquaintance invited him to a dinner meeting of the Full Gospel Business Men's Fellowship. He accepted, seeing it as an opportunity to promote his political views. Just in case there was conversation about the Bible, he put a New Testament in his pocket, "so I could counter their arguments."

He didn't hear political or theological speeches. "They threw a bucket of water on me. They told their life testimonies, how their lives were before and after Christ. One talked about how his wife was healed, and I began to laugh. 'God doesn't exist!' I thought."

The meeting concluded with prayer for the attendees to repeat. Herberth doesn't remember repeating it, but he does remember thinking on the way home that he should hedge his bets. If God didn't exist, there would be no judge at the end of life's road. But if God did . . . there was definite risk.

Arriving home, he knelt and prayed, "God, I don't think you exist, and if you do, you are thousands of miles away. If you are God, show me you exist. The day you show me, I will never stop telling people you are real." He prayed for his wife and children, and then he asked for help. He confessed his sins and asked, "Touch me. Change me.

"I sat on the bed and heard a voice that spoke audibly, called me by name, and said, 'Tell your wife that you love her.'

"Another voice said, 'She is asleep. Tell her tomorrow.'"

The first voice won.  He woke Ivet and instead of abusing her out of a drunken stupor, he touched her gently and said, "Ivet, I love you."

"She got up and hugged me. I began to laugh out loud and scream, 'I am free!' "

Intense Bible study followed, and gradually he began to live a life of that freedom. "In February, it will be fourteen years since I touched drugs, alcohol, or cigarettes."

As a member of the Somotillo Baptist church, he was selected by Pastor Diómedes Santeliz as one of several members to attend Community Health Evangelism (CHE) training at the Nehemiah Center. Of the eighteen people attending the initial training, just Herberth and Elizabeth Rodríguez continued with additional training.

And, when they stepped out to apply the training, El Ojoche was the first village they selected.

## Working in the Dirt with CHE

*Róger Pavón*

Originally put into place in Africa in the 1980s, the CHE program is now used internationally by nearly four hundred churches and organizations in more than one hundred countries to serve the physical and spiritual needs of people.

Nicaraguan native Róger Pavón is the Ezra team member who heads up this program for the Nehemiah Center. This Nehemiah Center program has been financed by Medical Ambassadors, now Global CHE Enterprises, and by CRWRC. Food for the Hungry has also performed important supportive roles.

An industrial engineer and chemist in his late forties, Róger first became aware of CHE while working for his denomination, Central American Mission. He had been working through his denomination trying—with little success—to encourage pastors to become more involved in their communities, when he first heard about CHE in the wake of Hurricane Mitch. In June 2000, he attended his first CHE workshop, and started to put the strategy into place in San Juan, a community in the Boaco region northeast of Managua.

As a founding board member for the Nehemiah Center, Róger introduced the center to the CHE concepts. In February 2002, he started working for the center, and today the Nehemiah Center has started CHE programs in sixteen communities. Through his denomination, Róger was instrumental in reaching another twelve communities.

What is CHE?

At its heart, CHE develops leaders and hope in communities that have neither.

It starts with CHE trainers, like Herberth, who go into communities to raise awareness of needs and opportunities. One of the key messages they stress is that CHE represents a way for the community to address its own physical, social, and spiritual needs: CHE is not a program that will offer money.

Success is only possible if the community both understands and is willing to take responsibility for its own problems.

Through a series of open meetings, the community decides for itself whether to undertake CHE as a community. If it decides to move forward, the community chooses its leaders, who are then trained for the work they will do. They learn about community organizing strategies, they receive specialized health training, and they learn about God's love for them and the importance of a relationship with him, with others, and with his world.

Once trained, these community leaders then choose other community members to be community health evangelists, who also receive specialized health-promotion training. (From among four hundred class options, they receive the training that is most appropriate for their situation.)

These volunteers hit the streets in a big way. These people learned how to improve the health of their own households, and work to pass along their new knowledge to their neighbors. In essence, they become personal health evangelists to their community.

"Our emphasis is development," said Róger. "When we go to the community, we tell them we are not going to give out food, clothes, or toys—not even build a clinic. We are going to help you develop your ability to change things through your own resources."

## Back in El Ojoche

*Street entrance to El Ojoche*

When Herberth and Elizabeth Rodríguez first began visiting El Ojoche and getting to know its residents, they started as volunteers, using public transportation or a taxi—paid with their own money. "We did it because we were in love with God and the ministry and wanted to apply the knowledge that we gained," said Herberth. Eventually they received donated motorcycles.

At the first formal meeting in El Ojoche, despite objections, the residents agreed to try the program. They selected a CHE leadership committee of seven to receive training. These seven learned about biblical worldview, preventative health, healthy interpersonal relationships, discipleship, leadership, organic agriculture, and more.

An easy road? Definitely not. Partway into the training, other community members got impatient. "You guys meet and meet and meet and train and train and train, but you don't bring us anything," they said to the CHE leaders.

Herberth and Elizabeth had warned leaders this would happen. "Don't worry. Let's keep moving ahead," Herberth told them. And they did.

In 2007, that hard work produced dramatic results. Hurricane Felix had ripped through the area in September, followed by persistent heavy rainfall and flooding. On the heels of the flooding came a tornado that devastated the fall harvest. When the rainfall stopped in October, the El Ojoche children and adults finally took to the outdoors. They didn't realize that the rainfall had facilitated an invasion of leptospirosis, bacteria generally found in water contaminated by animal urine. Inside of two weeks, 3,790 Nicaraguans were infected, and ten of them died.

When the outbreak began, El Ojoche leaders surveyed the community, tallying residents with even one disease symptom and teaching them how to avoid contracting leptospirosis—avoiding puddles, wearing boots, and so on.   When government health officials arrived, they were quickly able to transport and treat the thirty-nine infected El Ojoche residents. One, a teenager, died on the way to the hospital.

The Ministry of Agriculture ordered all infected livestock to be immediately killed and disposed of. But with a flurry of phone calls and collaboration with international agencies, the El Ojoche committee learned the livestock could be saved if immediately treated with Oxitet-raciclina. With the agreement of the Ministry of Agriculture and medicine transported by Food

---

### FROM CAROL'S JOURNAL
### *Helping That Hurts*

En route to El Ojoche, my driver and translator Nathan Sandahl tells me not all villages that have received Community Health Evangelism (CHE) training have changed as dramatically as the one I am about to see. Not all have taken the initiative to shape their own futures.

He tells me of his recent conversation with a resident of El Limonal, where he was taking photos of children as part of his work for Food for the Hungry. Seeing his camera, one mother began to dirty her son's face and clothing, convinced that the worse he looked, the more likely he would be to attract a sponsor.

"We fight a handout mentality," Nathan says. And handouts sometimes backfire.

He remembers a North American organization that picked a Nicaraguan location that needed latrines and built them, not consulting or building relationships with local people. When the team left, the residents used the latrines for grain storage instead. They were, after all, the best-built structures in the village.

"It is easy for North Americans to gather statistics and numbers—and produce quick results," he says. "They can have almost a God-complex."

As I keystroke notes in the back seat, my laptop screen propped against the seat in front to stabilize it as we bump along toward El Ojoche, I realize that heedless helping can indeed be hurtful—for both sides of a cross-cultural transaction. [1]

---

[1] *When Helping Hurts* is a book the Nehemiah Center recommends service-and-learning team members read before coming to Nicaragua. For publication details, see Appendix C.

for the Hungry, the community speed-
ily injected its horses, cows, and pigs
instead of killing them.

Public officials who visited the
community praised its leadership
and organization. They noted that the
disease would have spread much more
rapidly without the community's speedy
and organized response.

Today, the change is palpable in
El Ojoche—obvious in the look of the
community, and in the respect and self-
esteem evident in the eyes of its residents.

*El Ojoche Baptist church*

The streets are garbage-free, their
sloping sides edged with rocks to prevent
erosion. A schedule is posted publicly
on a metal sign listing who is currently
responsible for cleaning streets and
community areas.

In 2008, twelve residents traveled to another community to see how
to grow new varieties of fruits and vegetables in their yards. They learned how
to harvest water during the rainy season
for dry-season irrigation. Families drew
up plans to organize their yards, including vegetable gardens, trees for fruit and
firewood, and plants to prevent erosion.

Submitted photo

*El Ojoche water tank*

Now, instead of being littered with paper, cans, and bottles, El Ojoche's backyards are sprinkled
with fruit trees and gardens.

Together, residents also addressed its water problems. They organized and planned community water storage to tide them over during the dry season. They built latrines and wells. Child
mortality rates and the incidence of diarrhea and parasites in children began dropping.

After drilling several wells, community members still found themselves short of water. So,
late in 2008, they undertook a new initiative, the construction of large cisterns to catch rain-

FROM CAROL'S JOURNAL

### Riding Along
### for the Delivery

As we walk toward our vehicle, ready to leave El Ojoche, a pottery artisan asks if her twelve-year-old daughter can ride with us to deliver a large, lidded pot to a customer.

"Of course," Nathan Sandahl says.

She sits shyly on the back seat, pottery on her lap, its lid sporting a white ceramic flower. With Nathan translating, I ask the cost of the pot.

Twenty-five córdobas ($1.25), she says.

And how much time does it take for your mother to make it?

She and Nathan talk a bit and decide it takes one and a half hours of hands-on time over a three-day period of shaping, drying, and firing. Her mother usually processes three or four pots in tandem.

Two kilometers from El Ojoche, she exits our vehicle. She will deliver the pot, then walk back home.

Watching her shrink in the distance, I am disoriented by double vision. My North American eyes see an intolerable effort for a mere $1.25. My emerging El Ojoche eyes see a hope and a future.

water during the rainy season. They began by building two cisterns that held 100,000 liters of water each. Residents daily sweep their houses, bathe their children, and drink chlorinated water. In the past no student graduated from high school; now they have a trained community nurse.[1]

A decade ago, said resident Maria Gunera, she only occasionally sold a ceramic pot. Now, after many in the community have learned more about pottery making through the NicaMade program of Food for the Hungry, people from outside travel to the community to buy their pots.

"God was the first changer. It began with changing our hearts and minds. We found the unity and vision to work together to bring change," said Venancio Rios.

Despite their progress, they remain humble. "Our standard of living has changed greatly," said Virgilio Espinal. "We aren't necessarily above the communities around us, but we have become an example . . . And our roads are open so we can talk and share ideas with those needing help to improve their village situation."

The people of El Ojoche continue to have visions and dream dreams. The ceramic workers envision a pressure-fed kiln to improve their product even more. The com-

---

[1] It is also worth noting that the collaboration among nonprofit organizations that has worked so well elsewhere was evident in El Ojoche, too. Rotary Clubs, Food for the Hungry, CRWRC, and Nuevas Esperanzas were among the nonprofits that helped El Ojoche residents improve their village.

*El Ojoche town meeting*

munity map shows the planned locations for seven more cisterns to store water. Villagers dream of restoring the forests, of building stronger homes using local materials. They want to experiment with more plants in their gardens. But, added Virgilio, "it is in God's hands."

"You can't start a campaign without God. You go nowhere," said Alejandro Andrades, a community organizer. "Because of the CHE vision and the action of all in the community, we have overcome difficulties by joining forces in a common vision with short-term and long-term goals. With God's help we want to see El Ojoche with all basic services: potable water, less illness, greater integration of families—and community solidarity—a humble community with hospitality and service."

*Managua homes*

# 09

## Joining God in the Lowest Places

*Most of us fix meals and add salt. But we are the salt.*

- CARL MOST

Driving through Mateare, a town of about 27,000 residents twenty-five kilometers northwest of Managua, Carl Most stopped for Nixon Delgadillo. He was waiting on crutches and just one leg at his home across the street from a horse-drawn cart whose driver was talking on a cell phone.

Carl, a youth outreach staff member at the Nehemiah Center, shared oranges from his backyard with Nixon's mother, and sat with Nixon and his girlfriend in plastic chairs his mother brought from the house. She leaned against its cement blocks a few yards away as Nixon and Carl talked.

Nixon said he had been through a week of ups and downs adjusting to the loss of his leg. Carl, a 44-year-old New Zealand missionary with the shoulders of a weight-lifter and the jaw of a drill sergeant, listened with the attentiveness of a counselor.

Several months ago, Nixon and a friend had offended members of La Tufalera, a Mateare-area gang, when they opted out of a planned fight. When the pair said no and started to walk away, the others chased them with machetes. Nixon outran them, but his friend was caught. When they started beating his friend, Nixon ran back to help, fought off the attackers, telling his friend to run. As he fought them back, the gang rained machete blows on him. His life was saved when a neighbor fired a gun into the air, scaring off the attackers. An infection later developed in the leg that had been nearly severed, forcing doctors to amputate it.

*Nixon Delgadillo*

During his weeks in the hospital, to the joy of his Christian family, God touched Nixon's heart, and he joined them as part of God's family. In his subsequent testimony at a worship service, he told the congregation of his longing that God would also become Lord in the lives of his attackers.

Carl had stopped to provide Nixon with a ride to a Bible study meeting of former gang members. On this particular evening, they were studying Romans 12, "We are all part of the same body . . ." When Carl and Nixon arrived, there were complicated handshake rituals all around. "We are brothers of the street," they said.

The men carried red plastic chairs from the church across the street and set them up in a front yard. One of them raised a bare bulb on an extension cord with a forked branch and propped the branch against barbed-wire laundry line, flooding the area in yellow light. Women materialized out of the cement-block house, cloths in hand, and wiped the ever-present dry-season dust from the chairs. They selected oranges from the box when Carl offered them. "These are the last oranges from my orange tree. Now just pray that my avocado trees fill up!"

The group took seats, removed their caps, and prayed together. The twelve around the circle ranged in age from sixteen to thirty.

There was lots of joking and laughter, but when Nixon started talking about his week, silence fell and the men listened carefully, responded gently, sharing his pain. "Christian life is not just glory and hallelujah, but blessing also in the valleys," said Carl.

Laughter and joking resumed, along with an opportunity to recite memorized verses. For the member who memorized the most verses since the last meeting, there was a prize—a bag of rice. After the recitation of John 15:16 ("You didn't choose me. I chose you. I appointed you to go and bear fruit."), one member commented, "Many of us are the fruit of the labor of Francisco [the group's organizer] and Carl and others. But even though we are the fruit of their work, the glory is God's. It is not about us, but it is about God and his faithfulness."

Another member, not yet willing to surrender to God, told the group his marriage was in trouble and he and his wife fought often. If he became a Christian, he said, she would *really* be unhappy with him. Carl planned a visit to him the following week.

After the group had been studying Romans 12 for an hour, a young man entered the front yard, limping toward the house, supported on each side by a woman. The women sitting in the doorway listening to the Bible study provided him a seat and one of them massaged his ankle while his face registered obvious pain. The Bible study continued uninterrupted.

Later, as they wrapped up, the group discussed when to put a gravestone marker on the grave of Carlos  Cruz, a friend killed in a machete fight. Not wanting him to be in an unmarked grave, they raised the funds for a gravestone and wanted to place it together in his honor. Decision made, the meeting ended.

Founder and leader of the study group is Francisco Obregon. A former gang member, he had gotten into petty theft and alcohol abuse. When he became a Christian, he wanted to launch a ministry to area street gangs, but met resistance in his congregation. Then he attended a Nehemiah Center youth leader training in Chinandega in 2005. "It lit a fire under him," Carl remembered. "It provided him with a method." He started meeting with one of the worst gangs in the neighborhood, winning their confidence.

Francisco's original group had been larger, and some members were less committed than others. Following the Nehemiah Center leader-training model, he revised his tactics, and when one study session ended, he launched a smaller group of potential leaders—who could themselves become leaders and multiply in effectiveness. Carl Most came alongside him as his mentor, training him as he is training others.

"The goal of the Nehemiah Center's youth outreach is to train leaders like Francisco so that they will be changed in their personal lives, their families, and help to change their communities with a new vision, a new way of living," said Carl.

## Youth at Risk

In the United States, the term "youth at risk" frequently refers to teenagers who are at risk of dropping out of school. In Nicaragua, the term applies more to the youth who already spend most of their time on the streets, perhaps spending six, eight, ten hours a day outside of their homes. With fractured home lives, no jobs, and no recreation opportunities, it is easy

## Drug Trafficking to the End

Carlos Cruz had been involved in an initial larger Bible study group. At one point, he moved away from Mateare and moved back in with his mother in Managua. Thirty years old, he found it hard to handle her restrictions, such as 'Be home every night at eight.' He had no job and ended up trafficking drugs for an income. One day, while he was hanging out on an outdoor basketball court, friends demanded drugs from him. Carlos refused because he wanted to sell it to customers who would pay a better price. These so-called friends chased him. The situation quickly got out of hand, and they hit Carlos with their machetes. Francisco and others, who were there watching the game, carried Carlos off to a clinic. He was dead before he arrived.

*Walls and locked gates are common protection for homes and businesses.*

to see how youth can get into big trouble.

Most of them do not attend school, and they are at risk of both drug consumption and drug trafficking because of unemployment. Sex trafficking, prostitution, and sexual slavery are also risks.

Although crime in Nicaragua can't be entirely blamed on the youth, the effects of crime are obvious in the day-to-day lives of Nicaraguans. Women, like Lourdes Rivas in Chapter 6, generally do not wear valuable jewelry in public for fear of theft. Most homes have gates, guard dogs, and bars over their windows. It is common to hire a guard to watch over your vehicle when you park in a public place. The Nehemiah Center itself is a building behind a wall with a guarded gate.

The Nehemiah Center's programs are aimed to improve the situations of these youth, perhaps thirteen to twenty-five years old or more. The center's strategy is to develop youth leaders, generally on the older side of this age range, who will work directly with youth in their communities. Many of these youth leaders themselves come out of similar situations. Others simply have a heart for working with youth.

## The Journey to Mateare

*Carl Most*

In 2005, Carl Most was a man in transition. His time was ending with the mission organization with which he had originally come to Nicaragua, and he was looking for a new place to be used. At the same time, the Nehemiah Center was looking for someone to launch its youth outreach program.

A native New Zealander, Carl, his wife, Kathy, and their two children had been in Nicaragua since 1998. Prior to that, Carl had worked in youth formation in New Zealand for ten years.

Carl came to Christ in a youth Bible club at the age of twelve. Although his parents were not Christians, they allowed him to attend church. His teen years, he said, were rough. "My family disintegrated. There was violence and alcohol and all that." He lived with his father, attended a Bible college in New Zealand, worked in youth ministry for ten years, and then moved to Nicaragua in 1998.

In 2005, now with a different mission agency, the Caribbean Ministries Association, Carl joined the Nehemiah Center's youth ministry. "The Nehemiah Center knew my heart and thought I was a fit.

"It certainly was a God thing for me to join a mission agency [Caribbean Ministries] from the United States that valued what they saw in the Nehemiah Center and gave me trust and flexibility. I have been blessed with the freedom to explore without waving the flag of a single agency—for the good of the kingdom instead of a single mission."

Part of a three-person, youth-leadership-training team, Carl is the team's big-picture

FROM CAROL'S JOURNAL

## Nicaraguan Safety and Security

*Jairo Solano*

On my fourth Nicaragua trip, I need someone to explain Managua's ubiquitous armed security people, guard dogs, barbed-wire fences, and walls. Then, at the Nehemiah Center reception desk, I see Jairo Solano who works with Food for the Hungry.

Jairo was my chauffer for a trip to León last year. He is the perfect person to help me understand: a Nicaraguan who grew up in a middle-class Christian family, married a gringa, has lived in both the United States and Nicaragua, and—especially important for me—is fluent in English.

His first statement surprises me: Nicaragua has very little international drug trafficking, smuggling, kidnapping, or crimes like that. According to U.S. research, when it comes to organized crime, Nicaragua is the safest country in Central America.

Then he continues. Street crime is a different matter. Burglary and home break-ins are very frequent. So most houses in middle- to upper-class neighborhoods, need a security guard, coiled barbed wire, dogs, and electric fences. Alarm systems are a must.

Break-ins happen mostly during the day because at night thieves can't see as well, the owners are home, and the dogs are loose. During the day owners are at work, and the dogs are tied. Thieves jump in, and they steal whatever they can find—computers, televisions, cooking utensils, clothes, even shoes.

Jairo lives in a two-house area with a gate and guard. Recently thieves entered the adjacent house, which was unoccupied. They stole the electric breaker box, outlets, and light bulbs, but left Jairo's house untouched because his wife and children were at home. The stolen goods are often sold in what is known as the Oriental Market, a thirty-six-acre black market in the heart of Managua.

"What about the police?" I ask.

"We cannot rely on the police," he says. "They do not provide enough coverage. When our house was broken into, we called the police. They said they'd come in twenty minutes. They never came."

Sometimes police say they will be able to come if you can supply them with money for gas for the return trip. They do show up for serious crimes—if someone was killed—but for the theft of a propane tank, they will not come.

I ask about the houses of the poor, which have no walls. I speculate, "They are probably not at risk because they have so little."

"Oh, no," says Jairo. "They are at risk. They don't have walls because they cannot afford them. Someone might still come into their house, to steal even a pair of shoes and sell it at the market."

Then I remember seeing giant, skinny dogs in even the poor neighborhoods.

He adds, "If we can't rely on the police, we all have to provide our own protection." He explains that Managua, as a large city, has a higher need for guards and dogs and fences than smaller towns.

I have one more question. "Why is there so little organized crime in Nicaragua?"

Jairo says that statistics show a gang that tries to organize gets caught within two months. He laughs. "The reason is funny: We Nicaraguans are much too disorganized to organize crime!"

## Origins of the Youth Program

Funding for the Nehemiah Center's youth mission comes mostly from Caribbean Ministries, the mission with which Carl Most is associated. The essence of the content, however, originates with the Center for Transforming Mission (www.ctmnet.org). Christian Reformed World Missions (CRWM) and the Center for Transforming Mission (CTM) work together to spread this content (called Strategy of Transformation) in Latin America.

Today, in addition to Nicaragua, Strategy of Transformation training has been completed in El Salvador, Honduras, Guatemala, Dominican Republic, and Haiti—all made possible because of the alliance between CRWM and CTM. Joel Van Dyke, a CRWM missionary in Guatemala, heads up the training and personally helped lead the original round of training in Chinandega. However, since the start of the second cycle in León, Carl Most, Roberto Armas, and Hultner Estrada have been leading the training themselves.

person. Hultner Estrada is the master trainer and producer of materials, and Roberto Armas, who lives in León, is the person who stays in the most day-to-day contact with youth leaders in León. Carl comes from a Baptist background, Hultner and Roberto from a Pentecostal background.

Hultner grew up in a Christian home in Nicaragua and served in various roles in the church. His passion is evangelism. Even as a child, he wanted to tell people about Jesus. Before joining the Nehemiah Center as coordinator for youth at risk and arts and media, he worked for nine years in Christian radio. He also served as associate pastor for *Iglesia Cristiana Josué* (Joshua Christian Church) in Managua from March 2005 until April 2011.

Roberto also grew up in a Christian home in Nicaragua, was a youth leader in his church, and is currently a training assistant for the team. As a college student, he was active in *Comunidad de Estudiantes Cristianos de Nicaragua* (CECNIC), a campus Christian students' organization, which sent him to the first round of Nehemiah Center trainings. Trained as a biologist, his environmental work for the Nicaraguan government was ending when he learned of the Nehemiah Center's need for a youth leader trainer. He joined the youth team part-time in 2008.

The three are not only colleagues; they are also supportive friends. "We hold each other accountable and lift each other up. If it were not for that, we probably would not be here," said Carl.

## Roots of the Youth Ministry

The youth ministry was launched under the Nehemiah Center umbrella in 2005 with Caribbean Ministries as the chief funder and the Center for Transforming Mission as the original source for the training curriculum. The training curriculum is called the Strategy of Transformation. Its purpose is to equip grassroots leaders to serve at-risk youth and their families.

Earlier in 2005, Carl Most, Steve Holtrop, and others from the Nehemiah Center had attended a vision conference in Guatemala on the Strategy of Transformation. It was there in Guatemala that they learned about theology from below, a concept that, in essence, recognizes the worth of the faith experiences of suffering people. It's a complex concept, but it has been a powerful one for these leaders.

*From left, Nehemiah Center youth leadership training team: Roberto Armas, Hultner Estrada, and Carl Most*

"Grace is like water that flows and settles in the lowest places," said Hultner. "We try to read the Scripture through the eyes of those who live in those lowest places. It's not the same as me reading it from my pastoral position. They are facing so many problems and struggles, and life has crushed them so many times that good news for them sounds different."

Using Hagar as an example, Hultner explained the concept in more depth. Hagar, as we are told in the book of Genesis, was the handmaiden of Abraham's wife, Sarah. She bore Abraham a son, but later both Hagar and her son, Ishmael, were pushed out. "We respect and admire Abraham as a leader and as a saint. So, when we read the Hagar story, we identify with Abraham," said Hultner. "When the least read it, they read it through the eyes of Hagar and something changes.

"We have lots of Hagars who have been pushed out of their houses. Lots of women who had an undesired pregnancy, abuse, sexual slavery . . . Hagar was an outsider. Egyptian, not Jewish. But she is the first woman in Scripture who puts a name to God: the God who sees . . . Sometimes these outsiders have a better understanding of who God is. They get to a point of knowing God before we do."

Added Carl: "Hagar got to that point before Abraham did. That interpretation opens another door for us. We, as the body of Christ, need to learn from people outside the body of Christ and hear their stories and learn from their experiences."

In their ministry, these men see people who won't go near youth at risk, considering them cursed while God and his blessings are in the church. But the Nehemiah Center's youth strategy is different. "Grace from below is a theology of the cross," said Carl. "Your life will be blessed by being in the hard places, and you can join him there. God is already there and already at work.

"We started under the tutelage of guys outside of here [Nicaragua]," Carl said. "Now it's in our hands, and we are running with it: serving the least, the last, and the lost in difficult places. The journey is exciting and demanding."

## Youth Ministry: Nuts and Bolts of *Mision Transformadora* (Transforming Mission)

After spending six months in preparation, the youth leaders decided that Chinandega, an area with other transformation ministries already in place, was a fertile place to start.

They announced over the radio that a youth outreach course would be offered and also spread the word through their network of pastor and church connections. They didn't work hard at a broad outreach. They wanted people truly interested and committed.

The first cycle of training from June 2005 to 2007 in Chinandega was attended by 130 people, representing ten different denominations. About fifty completed the training.

After Chinandega they made revisions in the training curriculum and began a second cycle of training in León. Roberto Armas, one of the first students to complete the entire cycle of training, led the second round in León. In 2010, thirty-six core people graduated from the León training.

One revision made after the first round of training in Chinandega required participants to go out into the wider community, something they were afraid to do. They were afraid to cross the boundaries between the church and the community. In León, the trainees visited communities, completed community service, and led seed projects, using local resources.

For example, the leaders challenged the students to help youth in a rural community that had a very high youth suicide rate. They held soccer and basketball competitions, opening it with drama, dance, and messages. At the end of the competition, they returned and awarded trophies.

## Curriculum

"You cannot find the right answers until you ask the beautiful questions," said Carl. Most of the courses are not giving answers; they are asking questions.

The curriculum for the youth training program is intense, focused on making God pertinent to life on the street.

Although the curriculum first came from the Center for Transforming Mission, it has evolved through stages. "Our first manuals needed to be adapted for a more interactive learning style," said Hultner. "They also needed to be contextualized. The examples were very American, talking about the Cosbys and Simpsons, using words like 'ghetto,' and referring to North American music. We needed to use Nicaraguan stories, movies, and songs that taught the same thing."

Although Hultner does the hands-on work with the manual, the three function as a think tank in improving it and developing it.

The curriculum has eight sections, with a separate manual for each. Three sections are designed to strengthen students to work within the church. Five are geared toward working outside the church. Some examples of the topics:

- *In But Not Of.* How far is too far? We need to be the salt of the world. How far can we get without mixing with culture too much and without compromising our Christianity?

- *It Is a Family Affair.* Where in the Bible is a perfect family? And where in our world? They don't exist. But we make an idol of a perfect family and are weighed down by thinking every family ought to be like that. We waste our time trying to make a perfect family. The good news is that throughout the Bible, God's grace reaches families who are not perfect, just as ours are not perfect.
- *The City of God.* Seeing reality through the eyes of the Lord. Most of us think that the world is Satan's playground, but we need to confront that misunderstanding, that wrong vision. It is the Holy Spirit's playground. We need to see this reality and join the work of the Holy Spirit today.

## The Work and Impact Multiply

*Rodrigo Gámez*

In Poneloya, 120 kilometers northwest of Managua near the Pacific Ocean, Rodrigo Gámez has started a street ministry. He works midnight to 7 a.m. in a shrimp factory, eats breakfast, and heads to the streets until noon.

"Roberto, Carl, and Hultner brought me the light of knowledge," he said, seated on his father's front porch and topping his long and lanky frame with a Stetson. "They said, 'You want to evangelize? You need to relate to people where they are—playing baseball and basketball on the street corners.'

"So I took a basketball with me. They told me I played like Michael Jordan and asked me how to do that. I taught them, learned their names and pasts, went to their parties. One day I came with a basketball in my left hand and a Bible in my right. They said, 'You are a Christian? We behaved badly at those parties!' I said, 'No problem.' Day by day I told them Christ loves them, and I remained a good friend to them."

Before his training, Rodrigo said he went out with just a Bible and criticized people on the streets, telling them they were not Christians.

"Now I want to feel their pain, to cry with them, and tell them there is a way out—Jesus Christ.

"So, I sit with them and talk with them. When they tell me they are sick and have abandoned God, I say God hasn't abandoned them. I try to find the Goliath hindering them from coming to church.

"I show young people into alcohol and drugs the love of God without pressuring them. I not only talk, but I also listen."

Rodrigo can identify with street youth. The son of a Poneloya pastor, at twelve he took to the streets—drugs, alcohol, gangs. He told his father, Salomon, that God was only for very old people. He wanted to fight. "'The people in your church are doing nothing for God, nothing for the people in the streets,' I told him. 'When you preach, they sleep.'

"Then one day someone [not a family member] hugged me and said, 'I love you. You are important.' He talked to me about the love of God. My life started changing. I had wanted to be the center of attention, but the only real center of attention is Jesus Christ. I got to know him. And I told God I wanted to go to the streets to preach."

*Verónica Torres*

He didn't head for the streets immediately though, but led praise and worship for his father's congregation, *Iglesia Mi Redemptor* (My Redeemer Church). Training in the Nehemiah Center youth leadership program followed, and a street ministry.

Iglesia Mi Redemptor used to have thirty members. Now it has 120. On a typical Sunday morning, eighty of the worshippers are youth.

### Verónica

East of Poneloya, in León, Verónica Torres, a petite woman with a calm voice and demeanor, studied Nehemiah Center resources while recovering from spinal cord surgery. "Those materials transformed my vision," she said. "It became my vision to reach the places of most need."

She started working with young women who have been sexually abused, attempted suicide, or who supported themselves through prostitution. Her first step, in consultation with North Americans she had worked with, was to secure eleven sewing machines. Then she and an assistant visited poor neighborhoods and, with the help of an area psychologist, identified eighteen young women from just a four-block area, including a fourteen-year-old prostitute and an eighteen-year-old with four children. The goal: a collective where the young women could sew and embroider items to earn a living.

Sitting in her living room adjacent to a room crammed with fabric and sewing machines, she said, "When the girls say they are empty, it is our opportunity to share the gospel. The Nehemiah Center taught us to listen to them and what they want to share.

"Many of their parents don't care where these daughters are. Our goal is that the girls know Christ, and their families know him also."

Though supported by her husband, the church's pastor, Verónica encountered opposition from other church members who didn't share her passion for the youth at risk. The couple started another church in another area, and Verónica has resumed her passion there.

### Jackarelys

Jackarelys González, a Chinandega student, after one three-day training session, raised her hand to tell fellow class members about the course impact. "I planned to resign from my youth ministry job," she said. "I already had the letter written." But the course was providing her with new vision and ideas. "I was frustrated, but now I am energized," she said. A few months later, sent by her congregation, she and her husband launched a new church in Santa Matilde, a poor, rural community where many women supported themselves through prostitution. Now she and her husband pastor this new, growing church.

### Elias

Elias was sent to the training by his church in Nagarote. A former soldier, he ran his family like a military unit, and it was falling apart. A son had moved out to live with grandparents. Carl Most described his testimony after several sessions of training. "The war had affected Elias so much. He was not a man to cry, but the Lord broke his heart and he cried."

Carl's own eyes teared up as he continued to tell the man's story. "Elias told me that before reaching out to street kids, he needed to set things right in his own family. He went home and asked forgiveness from his wife and children. The Lord healed them and gave them a restored family to begin working with other youth in broken homes. He gave them a message!"

Seeing God on the streets is essential for these outreach workers.

"Without outreach, we don't understand who we are and why we are here," said Carl. "The church is the only organization that exists for the benefit of those who are not members. Outreach

## *Going Numb at Rostipollo*

*Chicken rotisserie at Rostipollo*

Jackarelys and Jairo enter Rostipollo with us hesitantly, gazing at the arched doorways, brick walls, and open-fire chicken rotisserie. A waiter pulls together several tables for our North American church team and these Santa Matilde co-pastors.

We have invited this young pastoral couple to lunch in a Chinandega restaurant following a visit to the church they started five years ago just a few miles away in Santa Matilde, a neighborhood of five thousand people known for its poverty, prostitution, alcoholism, drug use, and danger. They have told us about walking alongside the residents, of progress, and of plans.

As a university student, Jackarelys's goal was "to graduate and have a very good job working in a bank in a very nice dress.

"But the Lord dealt with me," she says. "I'm not in a bank in a very nice dress, but I am doing the Lord's will." She and Jairo have faced financial struggles and are living "one hundred percent by faith."

"The Lord takes really good care of us. We always have a meal on our table, and food and shoes," Jairo says. Today that meal is at Rostipollo, what appears to me to be a middle-of-the-road chain restaurant that specializes in chicken.

As soon as we are seated, Jackarelys takes a cell phone call, talks animatedly for a moment, then says goodbye. Studying the menu, she tells us the call was from her father. She has just astounded him by telling him she is at Rostipollo. "When I told him, he said, 'You're WHERE!?'"

With their two toddlers, she and Jairo have biked past this restaurant many times—their entire family of four on one bicycle, their only vehicle. And they have never, ever thought they'd be able to eat here. Rostipollo was only for rich people.

And now, here they are. And they are grateful.

Our translator Alma Hernández exchanges a few additional words with them in Spanish, while we seven North Americans struggle in silence to process what we have just heard. We fail.

A week later, I still fail.

Even now, a dozen or more restaurant meals later, whenever I return in memory to that Rostipollo table, I am awed by their commitment, struck dumb by their honesty, and shocked by the disparity.

That's the table to which Jackarelys and Jairo bring me.

And I am grateful.

is not something we add to our lives; it is the reality of who we are."

Hultner's vision of the church's mission has shifted. "I thought that people must come inside the church. I had the vision that a powerful church would be a magnet to the community. But now I understand that it is the very opposite. God had to wipe out the Tower of Babel so that it would spread out. Now I see that we need each other. We need our community and they also need us."

*Hultner Estrada*

Roberto once viewed a church's outreach only in terms of large evangelical campaigns. "I thought the gospel was just for people who came to church. I came to understand that God is a lot more than that.

"Before this, I saw an alcoholic in the gutter as refuse, as the filth of society. But I have learned that God loves even prostitutes and thieves. Jesus walked among the people and had relationships with all people."

Suffering has become more a part of Carl's thinking. "There is a time for glory, but it is only by way of the cross," he said. "However, most of us would rather bypass the cross and get to the hallelujah."

*Roberto Armas*

As he continued to speak, Carl's voice got softer; his words became slower. "We are surrounded by churches, yet there is no place I would rather be than right here among the people in hard places. God is more often in the streets than the sanctuaries. He is more real. More present. More powerful."

He paused as his eyes grew wet again. "There is a form of godliness in churches that denies power. I don't say that with bitterness, but with love. I was like that. This last chapter of our lives has been pretty powerful." Tears streamed down his cheeks. And there was a long silence in the room.

"It is life shattering," Carl concluded. "We teach that God is one who shatters images—*iconoclasta.* I am sure he is shattering over and over again our understanding of who he is and what he is about, little by little shaping us into the right vision and mission."

## Struggling into the Future

Although the three youth leaders have heard many stories of personal transformation, they still see less institutional and community change than they would like. They understand the obstacles that the youth leaders face. Like Verónica, some face hurdles within their own churches when ministering beyond the church walls.

They also struggle with having the time to personally follow up with and mentor new youth leaders. Staying in touch is hard—leaders lose cell phones or sell them and it is hard to get in touch.

It is difficult for them to leave their work in a city where there is not yet a cross section of trainers in place who can work together as their own team does at the Nehemiah Center.

At the same time, the three leaders are reaching a better understanding of how their work fits into other Nehemiah Center initiatives such as the goal for healthy churches—churches that could help care for the youth in their communities.

They hope to see solid teams in place in Chinandega and León that can continue multiplying the strategy of transformation on their own initiative.  Also on the agenda is starting the same cycle of training in Esteli, a city a couple hours north of Managua. They want to make more resources available to the trainers as well, DVDs with PowerPoint presentations, for example.

They also dream of adding a woman to the team—half of the people they train are women.

They realize, though, that their work is only part of the answer to Nicaragua's problems.

---

FROM CAROL'S JOURNAL

### *Energized*

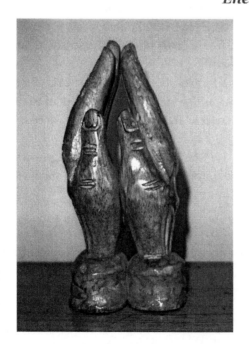

*Wood carving on Nehemiah Center desk*

When my interview began with the three leaders of the Nehemiah Center's youth program, Carl Most paused and said he would like to begin with prayer. He led.

After a four-hour marathon of talking, translating, and keystroking, we move to the Nehemiah Center lobby where I take their photo. I am turning to leave, when Hultner Estrada stops me. "Could we pray for a blessing and anointing on Carol for her work?" We form a circle, Carl places a hand on my shoulder, and Hultner prays for a blessing and the Holy Spirit's anointing on the creation of the book.

My voice softer and slower than usual, I respond, "I have already felt that anointing. Never before in my life have I been able to focus for four hours of interviewing."

Then, North American that I am, I add, "Maybe the Nicaraguan coffee helped some, too."

We laugh and then head for our different corners of the Kingdom.

So, as they move ahead, they will continue to look for where God is already at work, and come alongside of what is already happening.

It is as Carl summed it up: "God is working so beautifully in Nicaragua. It is our joy to be able to join him in this work."

*Ranchón at Nicaraguan oceanside restaurant*

# 10

## Tugged in Different Directions

*This arts camp helps the kids to look for healthy friendships. In the communities, they see a lot of violence, and have a lot of negative influences. But in the arts camp they see people who love them.*

*- HULTNER ESTRADA*

On the first day of arts camp, fifty kids—some eager, some shy, and all more than a little uneasy—each boarded a bus in front of their homes. The bus drove them to Amor Viviente, a church in the city of Chinandega.

What would the day bring? What would they do? And, worst of all, what if they couldn't do what they were asked to do? Would someone get mad at them? Their fears built with every kilometer.

As soon as the children stepped off the bus, friendly artists and assistants greeted the children, welcoming and valuing them.

That very first day, the students learned a song about being special.

*El Limonal arts camp participants show off photos of themselves with their teachers.*

"When we sang that song the first time, they looked at each other and were not able to feel they were special. We asked, 'Who is special here?' And none of them answered," recalled one of the teachers. "During the week they learned the song. By the last day, when we asked who was special, they raised their hands and yelled, 'We are! We are!' "

There is no teaching of the arts in the public schools; this camp was the children's only experience. For three or four hours a day, they studied and experienced visual arts, music, or movement. They learned art-making techniques, musical notes, rhythm, dance positions, and color combinations. They learned team work, perseverance, and hygiene. They also learned to hope, to encourage each other, and to feel valued.

Children learned to put brushes, pencils, and paints back into their correct places. They learned to wash their hands before snack time. They learned to work in teams and encourage each other—even children from other communities. They learned to trust their teachers. They learned to keep going through dance steps over and over before mastering them.

A success? Yes, the arts camp was definitely a success. But that week-long success took place after a couple years of struggles. And, the impact—though hopefully noteworthy in the lives of the children who attended—could have been so much more. Only one-eighth of the kids who wanted to attend were selected.

Throughout its short history, the Nehemiah Center has had its challenges. Developing healthy marriages, healthy churches, healthy communities, and improving the lives of youth always have been challenges and will continue to be. The programs will evolve as strategies are replaced by more successful ones, and as missionaries and trainers as well as funding sources come and go. Still, Nehemiah leaders are encouraged to see real transformation in the lives and communities of many they touch through these programs.

In a few areas, however, the Nehemiah Center has foundered. The arts, media, business development, communication—these are all areas in which the Nehemiah Center has had its struggles. Nehemiah leaders haven't given up, and after various setbacks, are employing new strategies they hope will sprout bigger rewards in the future.

## Arts and Media

When the Nehemiah Center launched its arts and media program in 2005, setbacks were at first more common than successes.

The initial goals were admirable—to develop a Christ–centered worldview in media and the arts, to create networks of Christian artists, and to produce transformational audiovisual materials. At the same time, center leaders hoped it would be another way to reach out to youth.

"We wanted to gain back the attention of Nicaraguan people, presenting something different than just yelling Scripture," said Hultner Estrada, who led the program.

Hultner and four Nehemiah Center volunteers met with artists and media people, then offered three workshops on art, media, and worldview. But, their vision never was achieved.

For one thing, networking between artists and media people failed to develop. The two groups had different interests and little to connect them. For another, the training lacked continuity—different people attended each session. And third, funding was in short supply.

For a time, Hultner and Kim Freidah Brown (FH missionary) continued to work with artist networks. In October 2007, the center hosted a choral music colloquium attended by twenty-five choral directors and members from the Managua area. In October 2008, the Nehemiah Center in collaboration with BuildaBridge (a nonprofit arts education program) hosted a conference attracting forty Christian artists as preliminary training for working with children's arts camps.

But in 2010, Kim returned to the United States. And, by this time, Hultner, who was hired as an Ezra team member to spend a quarter of his time on the arts program and three-quarters with youth, was finding that the youth programming demanded most of his time.

In the end, when funding became available, Hultner and Alicia Hamming of Christian Reformed World Missions (CRWM) who volunteered her time working outside of her primary role, made the camps happen. They recruited teachers from artists who had attended the earlier training. The network of artists had not developed the way Hultner had hoped, but it had served a different purpose.

In 2009 with the collaboration of the Nehemiah Center, Food for the Hungry, and Managua artists, fifty children from the tough urban slums of El Limonal and Bayardo Arce attended *Campamento de Artes,* a four-day arts camp for children at Amor Viviente church in Chinandega. In December 2010, the church worked with eleven artists to host a second camp, this time five days long for seventy-five

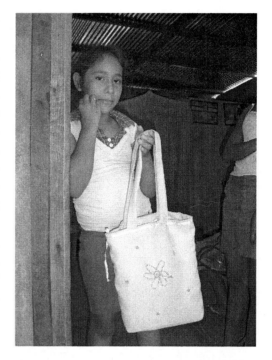

*Bayardo Arce girl holds satchel created at arts camp.*

Submitted photo

*Kim Freidah Brown and arts camp student entertain the rest of the group.*

### FROM CAROL'S JOURNAL
## *A Walk through Bayardo Arce*

*A mother walks with her daughter down the street in Bayardo Arce.*

After hearing about the arts camp, seven members of my church team and several coordinators pile into a van and head to Bayardo Arce, a neighborhood south of Chinandega that was created for people displaced by Hurricane Mitch. Also with us are members of three Chinandega churches considering arts camps as part of their neighborhood outreach.

Arriving, we dismount under a hot sun onto dirt streets and crowd against a barbed-wire fence hung with laundry to make way for a horse-drawn cart filled with recycled tiles. Only when it has passed can we begin our visits to families of arts camp students.

After his mother has unstacked a half-dozen plastic chairs to seat the majority of us around the front door of their two-room home, a boy tells us about learning to draw at the arts camp, about making new friends. His mother adds that he used to be withdrawn and speak little. Now he talks with her and with neighborhood children. She is grateful, she says, for the camp and the changes that have resulted. She is sorry they don't have samples of his art work. They have shared them with relatives living in other cities.

We wait in the shade of a plantain tree for another student to finish bathing. A parakeet perches on a nearby wire. Hair still wet, this student proudly shows us her drawings. Again, the best have been sent to family elsewhere. Her mother says the sketchbook and crayons are prized possessions that are carefully kept out of reach of siblings and neighborhood children.

We step over laundry water trickling street-side from a recent water toss and stop at another home. This student is shy—her mother is not home, but she gets the sand-filled water bottle she made at camp and shakes it in a rhythm she learned as we sing *Alabare* (Hallelujah). Her sister shows us a hand-embroidered fabric purse, also made at the camp.

At one stop, a camp participant leans on the fence and sings for us a song from camp, as younger siblings compete for our attention from inside a wooden-carton playhouse. At each stop we see broad smiles and hear about benefits—improved self-esteem, satisfaction in accomplishment, teaching other children what was learned. Their enthusiasm—like that of the coordinators we heard earlier—is overwhelming. So is their sense of hope.

As we return to the van—one of us already red with emerging sunburn—the cart drivers are trying, with little success, to convince the horse to back the cart of tiles onto a neighborhood yard.

Looking out the window, my husband remarks, "It's not the obvious poverty that bothers me as much as the lack of opportunity."

"Amen," I think.

Inspired by the hope I've heard, I recommit to raising funds for the arts camps for another year.

children from three communities. The children spent time with music (rhythm and singing), dance, visual arts, and sewing.

The children, ages eight through twelve, were selected based on their interest and aptitude for music, drawing, or dance, and their socio-economic need. "We looked for kids who urgently needed intervention or therapy through art-making so they could find hope, relaxation, and self-esteem," said Hultner.

Just a month after the second camp, those who attended and the four hundred not selected to attend started asking if there would be another camp next year.

Good question.

There are many difficulties to work through. As successful as they were, an expanded future for the arts camps remains uncertain. The artists-teachers were volunteers from

---

FROM CAROL'S JOURNAL

### *Bend in the Road*

This morning as our North American team of seven hammered out six pillars for a companion relationship with five Chinandega churches, I had not expected to come away with a fleshed-out plan, but we did. I was excited about its potential.

Now, over lunch at a Chinandega Chinese restaurant, we are meeting for the first time with pastors of our local companion churches. We tell them about Faith church, and they tell us about their congregations. When the discussion turns to potential areas of collaboration, we mention sponsoring arts camps for their neighborhood children.

Yesterday we saw the impact of Food for the Hungry's arts camps for children in Bayardo Arce, a Chinandega slum, and the plan we hammered out this morning includes ongoing sponsorship of those camps. So, we ask these pastors about collaborating on these arts camps.

They are hesitant. Seeing neighborhood children for just one week would not be ideal. They would prefer some sort of year-round program.

I'm taken aback, disappointed. We have such a beautiful plan. I can picture these congregations building the same hope and self-esteem that we have seen in Bayardo Arce. The conversation moves on, but I am stuck in disappointment at this roadblock.

As our van heads back for the hotel, I mention my disappointment to team member Harley Janssen, and he sees the resistance differently. He says, 'I wasn't surprised at all. I expected it.' Harley, at home in the world of corporate negotiation, sees the conflicting viewpoints as a necessary part of healthy negotiation.

As I listen to Harley, I remember earlier conversations with Nehemiah Center staff about the need for local ownership and for a balance of power.

What I saw as a roadblock is just a bend in the road and, I now realize, a sign of healthy churches and a healthy beginning to a relationship.

### FROM CAROL'S JOURNAL
## *God's Smugglers*

I'm going through customs on my first Nicaragua trip, along with other members of the service-and-learning team from my home church in Pella, Iowa. Stowed in each of our suitcases—wrapped in our clothes and in baby blankets or diapers for Nicaraguan children—is $25,000 in media equipment for the Nehemiah Center.

Our goal: get through customs with our suitcases unopened. If they are opened, however, each of us has a certified letter detailing the media pieces we carry and verifying that they are a donation to Food for the Hungry, a Nehemiah Center international nonprofit agency recognized by the Nicaraguan government.

As a second backup, a bilingual Nicaraguan lawyer is waiting just beyond customs to come to our aid if necessary. He is ready to point out to customs officers that the contents of our suitcases are all in keeping with customs laws, in case a customs officer tries to confiscate something or hassles us in hopes of a bribe.

To avoid attracting attention, we have taken off our team T-shirts and all have entered different customs lines, posing as individual tourists.

When the customs officer beckons, I take a deep breath and nonchalantly approach the counter. He glances up to see if I match my passport photo, takes my $5 fee, tells me to pass, and beckons the next person in line.

The same happens to each member of the team. "All those prayers were answered!" says one member as we load our suitcases into the waiting van.

I suppose so.

Except that—I'm embarrassed to say—a piece of me has been really hoping for a little drama. Back home, it would have made such a good story.

Managua, and had to leave their homes and work for a week to volunteer. Expanding the camps with those same teachers probably isn't an option, but identifying artists in Chinandega and training them to teach is a cumbersome task—both in terms of time and funding.

In February 2011, representatives from Chinandega, Nicaragua, and Pella, Iowa, churches visited Bayardo Arce families who had participated in the camp the previous month. Convinced of the value of the camps, the Pella team from Faith Christian Reformed Church committed to raise enough funds to hold one arts camp in 2012. Chinandega pastors saw great value for their neighborhoods, but preferred to create a year-round program—a more challenging undertaking. At press time, their future involvement had not yet been defined.

In short, the future for the arts camps has many options and many uncertainties.

Those uncertainties in the art outreach programs run parallel to issues that the Nehemiah Center has faced in its media programs.

Improving its media outreach carries several potential benefits. It could, of course, enable Nicaraguans to discover a new talent or perhaps, ultimately, a new career. It could prove to be another way for the Nehemiah Center to reach out to youth. It could prove to be a great way to improve collaboration with North American college students and Nicaraguans.

And, it could be a successful method for the Nehemiah Center to spread the word about its mission.

The possibilities are expansive, but, for various reasons, the program hasn't yet blossomed.

One of the few air-conditioned rooms at the Nehemiah Center houses $25,000 in media equipment, funded by Christian Reformed World Missions and Trinity Christian College of Palos Heights, Illinois. In Nicaragua heat and humidity, air-conditioning is crucial for the longevity and functioning of the equipment.

Since then, the media program has explored several options. "We are struggling to define ourselves," said Dave Stienstra, media coordinator. "Commitment levels have varied." Dave, a CRWM missionary who previously taught at the Nicaragua Christian Academy, joined the Nehemiah Center the same month that the video equipment arrived.

Several North American colleges have sent classes of media students to the Nehemiah Center for a semester. Sponsored by Trinity Christian College, the off-campus semester in filmmaking includes students from Calvin College and Cornerstone University, both in Grand Rapids, Michigan. Students experience life in a community and make a documentary as part of the semester. [1]

Twelve Nicaraguans have been trained in basic media skills. The Nehemiah Center sometimes produces short videos, both for the Nehemiah Center and for other Nicaraguan ministries.

A recent development that shows promise is the creation of participatory videos in which communities in development are trained to create their own documentaries. According to Insight-Share, a United Kingdom/France-based company with twenty years' experience in participatory video (PV): "PV can initiate a process of analysis and change that celebrates local knowledge and practice, while stimulating creativity both within and beyond the community."[2]

In other words, the Nehemiah Center hopes that communities, by participating in creating their own documentaries, will come together in ways they otherwise never would have. Communities learn more about themselves—their problems and their successes—and community leaders are identified. In this case, it is as much the making of the video as the showing of the video that constitutes the opportunity.

So far, this was worked well. Since early 2010, Dave Stienstra and Farid Román, a member of the Mateare youth group (see Chapter 9), have taken Nehemiah Center media equipment to three developing agricultural communities where CRWRC is working with Nicaraguan non-governmental organizations (NGOs). Over the course of a week, the two men trained the communities in basic camera and filming techniques, creating open-ended questions, interviewing, storyboarding, and editing.

---

[1] See the Nehemiah Center Film Channel (www.youtube.com/user/estudiocn) for an example of a student's work.

[2] Nick Curtis and Chris Lunch, *Insights Into Participatory Video: A Handbook for the Field*, InsightShare, London, February 2006.

"We are enabling them to measure their growth and empowering them to make their own documentary," said Dave. "To do that, they need to reflect on their own story—where they have been and where they are now. It also provides the opportunity to cast their vision for their future—where they would like to be and what they can work on."

Participatory videos have value both inside and outside of the communities making them. Communities become more self-aware; they see more clearly where they have been, where they are, and where they would like to go. Other communities who view these documentaries can learn from their failures and be inspired by their successes.

## Business Program Ups and Downs

Managua street vendor

As the second poorest country in the Western Hemisphere, Nicaragua has a critical need for economic opportunity. Forty-eight percent of the population is below the poverty line.[3] Due to a dearth of jobs, many Nicaraguans try self-employment with a small business. Few of them, however, understand Christian principles for a business, much less the details of managing one.

In the fall of 2001, the Nehemiah Center began working with a Nicaraguan organization of Christian business people. However, when these Nicaraguans met with North Americans, both had frameworks they could not set aside. According to Joel Huyser, the Nicaraguans wanted to discuss international politics, and the Americans expected to look at business plans in order to make loans. The Nicaraguan group eventually disbanded.

Meanwhile, in collaboration with Partners Worldwide, the Nehemiah Center had developed a training curriculum for the many self-employed micro-business people who populate evangelical churches in Nicaragua. A typical business person might be a single mother who makes tortillas in her home and sells them in the neighborhood or a woman who buys fresh fruits and vegetables from farmers and sells them in a small stand along the road.

The Nehemiah Center developed training materials that taught both kingdom values and simple, practical business skills. The purpose was to work with groups of micro-business people in churches and help them to write a business plan. These business people could then use their busi-

---

[3]A 2005 estimate. *CIA World Factbook: Nicaragua*, updated Dec. 13, 2010, <www.cia.gov/library/publications/the-world-factbook/geos/countrytemplate_nu.html> (January 7, 2011).

ness plans to apply for loans to the many micro-finance organizations in Nicaragua. As the businesses grew, they might eventually work with Partners Worldwide, an organization that focuses on small to medium-sized businesses and could provide mentoring, collaboration, networking, and possible financial assistance.

*Bob Vryhof*

The Nehemiah Center had the expertise to train Nicaraguans both in biblical worldview and also in basic business skills, according to Bob Vryhof. The Partners Worldwide regional facilitator for Latin America, Bob has been in Nicaragua since 2004 and has walked with the Nehemiah Center business program through its ups and downs as closely as anyone.

Initially it seemed that the program's key concepts were well understood—but in hindsight perhaps these concepts weren't as well understood as they should have been. One of the principles of the program was that the Nehemiah Center could provide training but any actual loans would need to come from other organizations.

It was necessary that Nicaraguans understand and take ownership of their business ideas, that they learn, and train, and do the hard work to make the businesses successful. That, however, is somewhat counter to Nicaragua's culture. Because of Nicaragua's history of need and its culture of dependency, many Nicaraguans naturally have an expectation of financial aid, perhaps even a sense of entitlement.

As Bob said, "People from developing countries think they are going to get access to money, especially when foreigners are involved. It is inevitable."

It was this expectation, below the surface and then highly visible, that brought difficulty. "The Nehemiah Center was always very clear about not giving loans," Bob remembered. "But they also recognized that as a very real need."

Initially, the program was a success. More than five hundred Nicaraguan micro-entrepreneurs were trained on biblical values and created business plans.

"The business training seemed to light a fire in a lot of places," said Bob. "We were seeing numbers of people who started coming and kept coming. There was impact! We would hear these people talking about margins increasing or inventory management being more efficient." It seemed that the training was having an impact even without loans.

Then came the complication: A small group of people in each city had the expectation of getting more. They concluded perhaps someone was holding out on them. Financial aid wasn't coming in through this program, and there was resentment.

"A small but loud minority can sway the rest," said Bob, "or perhaps talk so loudly that they are the only voices heard. Whatever the cause—all of a sudden, there was really poor communication."

Although the Nehemiah Center itself did not—and never intended to—provide loans, there was some thought the Nehemiah Center could train some small business owners to do what they needed in order to gain loans. However, the center never actually got to that training.

Some Nicaraguans may have felt entitled to loans, after having gone through so much business training. Or, perhaps, in the alphabet soup of international nonprofit organizations, they didn't realize the funding organizations were totally separate from the Nehemiah Center.

Some loan applicants turned in business plans with just three words in each blank. "That doesn't work anywhere on the globe," said Bob. "But it was a heavy blow [for the Nicaraguans to find out differently] when they assumed they deserved it and had earned it." To make matters worse, the Nicaraguans didn't have a broad enough business exposure to understand the big-picture process by which business decisions are made.

Maybe if the program hadn't grown so fast, or maybe if the Nehemiah Center had listened better to the minority voices, or maybe if the Nehemiah Center's loosely organized accountability structure had been tighter, the outcome would have been different.

In any case, however, in the fall of 2009, the business program went on hold for a year and a half. In February 2011, the Nehemiah Center hired Freddy Méndez to fill a part-time position. Nehemiah Center leaders are praying that filling this position will bring healing and new energy for the business program. It is far too early to tell how successful this will be in the future, but initial feedback indicates that Freddy is being well received. However, as of press time, long-term funding for this program had not yet been found.

## Focus to the Future

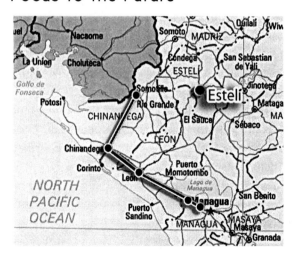

*Past focus: the corridor to Somotillo. Future focus: Esteli.*

Over the years since its beginnings in 1999, the Nehemiah Center has evolved. For one thing, it has become more focused.

In 2003, the Ezra team had projects in each of the five regions of the country. Only the sparsely populated Caribbean Coast was excepted. In 2004, realizing that it needed to narrow its focus in order to gain momentum, it opted to concentrate its efforts along the Pan-American Highway corridor that runs northwest through Los Brasiles, Nagarote, León, Chinandega, and up to Somotillo.

The planned strategy was for Ezra staff to train area leaders. These leaders would become agents of transformation in their institutions (schools, churches, and businesses). These institutions would band together and work for the transformation of the entire community. The plan was to complete that work in 2009—relying on local leaders to continue the mission so that the Nehemiah Center could shift efforts to a new area.

*Esteli is known in Nicaragua for its murals.*

Between 2004 and 2009, however, Nehemiah Center staff learned much about community development in cities. While staff members met with some success in smaller communities like Los Brasiles and El Ojoche, they learned that transforming larger cities was a much bigger challenge.

"We can't expect the same thing to happen in a city like León as in a small town such as El Ojoche," said Joel Huyser. "Small towns are ideal for development. People know each other. There are established leaders. If the community pulls together, they see real change. Doing that in a city like León is more difficult than we had originally thought, and it takes longer. There just aren't many models for this kind of work. New methodologies are needed, and we are discovering them as we go."

In February 2010 during a scheduled triennial assessment, a team of outside evaluators from Christian Reformed World Relief Committee (CRWRC), Christian Reformed World Missions (CRWM), and Food for the Hungry (FH) concurred with Joel's assessment. The program has yielded sufficient change on a personal level and some changes on an institutional level, such as in churches and schools, the funders' report concluded. But, it went on to note, examples of community-level changes are fewer, especially outside of the rural communities.

Therefore, the Nehemiah Center plans to maintain a supportive presence along the Pan-American corridor as necessary, and is leaning toward a more focused approach in new areas. For 2011 to 2015, the center plans to start in Esteli, the next big town east of the Pan-American corridor.

A city of more than 100,000 people a couple hours north of Managua, Esteli is bordered by a highway on the east and the Esteli River on the west. At an elevation of about 2,600 feet, the city is fairly pleasant year-round. Outside of the city to the west is home to tobacco growers and cigar rollers who make cigars known the world over. Inside the city are widely varied neighborhoods, some quite poor. Esteli is considered the agricultural hub for many of the farmers, cattle ranchers,

*Center director Daniel Boniche, working on plans and strategies at the Nehemiah Center*

and others who surround the city.

Using what they have learned working in León and Chinandega, Nehemiah Center leaders already are working in Esteli with an improved structure and sequence. In the first phase, seventy Esteli leaders were trained in biblical worldview and family relationships. In stage two, these leaders are forming networks of pastoral couples. Additional training is planned on healthy churches, youth leadership, and Community Health Evangelism. The goal: develop a repeatable process that can be used in other cities over the years, perhaps even by other organizations.

"So far, the response has been tremendous," said Nehemiah Center staffer Steve Holtrop. "People have been coming to our monthly meetings from as far inland as eight hours. More people want to come, but we have had to cap the attendance. The pastors' network has the same problem—too many pastors and wives want to join; we can't handle them."

In Esteli and other cities, the Nehemiah Center envisions the local churches—working in collaboration—as the agents for city-wide transformation. And, in fact, there has been some collaboration in the cities in which the Nehemiah Center has worked, made possible through the healthy church training and pastoral networks.

However, interdenominational collaboration has been more challenging to implement than expected, said Nehemiah Center Director Daniel Boniche. In León and Chinandega, for instance, the Nehemiah Center seeks to transfer the leadership in transformation work to the churches; however, those churches still feel a need for ongoing mentoring and encouragement.

One option being explored to help with ongoing support is long-term companion relationships with North American churches. In August 2009, the Nehemiah Center opened this possibility with a proposed "Woman at the Well" program.

Through this program, the Nehemiah Center hopes that North American churches and Nicaraguan churches will establish five-year relationships that "engage the heart, the head, and the hands of both churches." It challenges churches in both countries to grow together in their understanding of the church as a mission and jointly make a significant impact on the lives of marginalized people in their communities, particularly women and children. North American church members agree to travel to their Nicaraguan companion churches at least three times in five years, and both churches agree to share information, photos, and prayer requests. In addition,

Nicaraguan churches must complete a one-year healthy church training program (see Chapter 6).

In January 2011, three North American churches had committed to this five-year relationship, each of them in the Christian Reformed denomination: Faith Church of Pella, Iowa; Faith Church of Burlington, Ontario, Canada; and Immanuel Church of Hamilton, Ontario, Canada.[4] The program is brand new, and these churches are breaking new ground as they forge ahead, excited but also uncertain.

In addition to targeting the need to improve community-wide transformation, the 2010 assessment team report recommended the Nehemiah Center improve its communication. And again, Nehemiah Center staff agreed.

*Joel Huyser at the Nehemiah Center kiosko*

The communication challenge is partly one of staffing. The communications staff position has been empty since Pamela Neumann returned to the United States in May 2009. Pamela had raised her own funding for her position. With no replacement staff person, her work producing Nehemiah Center newsletters and updating its Web site has stalled.

The open-hallway and courtyard structure of the Nehemiah Center facilitates collaboration and informal exchange of information, but even so, staff members still know less than ideal about what's happening in the work of other team members in the country.

"Too often the right hand doesn't know what the left hand is doing. And I am at loss to figure out why," said Joel Huyser.

For example, when a team from Burlington, Ontario, Canada, told Steve Holtrop in its debriefing session of the powerful impact of meeting Verónica and learning about her work with former prostitutes, he wished the Nicaraguan agents of transformation trained by the Ezra team could have heard the story also. "At the moment, they don't come together unless we bring them together," Steve said. He is encouraged, however, by the excellent communication that he sees is beginning to happen in the networks of Christian schools.

A related question that Nehemiah Center collaborators wonder about from time to time is the relative merits of a centralized versus a decentralized organizational structure. Decentralization allows for freedom, creativity, and faster forward movement. On the other hand, a tighter organization offers more accountability. Under Joel Huyser's initial leadership, the Nehemiah Center

---

[4]Although not formally part of this program, Bethel Christian Reformed Church, Edmonton, Alberta, Canada, has had an ongoing relationship with several Nicaragua churches for more than ten years. Steve Holtrop said he considers them "grandfathered in" to the program.

*Mark Vanderwees in his Nehemiah Center office*

began with a decentralized structure. "As a member of a law firm, I was accustomed to a loose structure in which staff members are proactive, professional, and have independent decision-making authority." He acknowledged, however, "That does not work for all people and in all circumstances."

CRWRC's Mark VanderWees concurred. "We are a very loose organization. That is partly good, because it promotes creativity. But there is a down side when things break down from time to time. When new staff members arrive, how do you pull them in so they have a common mindset? New people need to be trained and supervised."

That is a very real question. The organizers of the Nehemiah Center developed their shared vision over years. They developed their relationships first, then developed the ideas that became the Nehemiah Center. But when new volunteers and new staff members come in—especially into key positions—how do you transfer and communicate in a short time what has taken years to come to fruition?

As new funding organizations come to Nicaragua, how does the Nehemiah Center welcome them while at the same time convey that it has a new model that those organizations have never encountered before? After all, it is only natural for organizations to both control and direct their funding and programming rigidly. To satisfy and attract donors, organizations feel the need to take credit and the need to report exactly what improvements were made with their money. They may fear that collaboration dilutes their "brand identity" and thus their ability to raise funds. Similarly, organizations naturally want to implement programs using methods they have already used in other countries.

"In its extreme, the international agency comes to see the local partner, such as the Nehemiah Center, as the implementer of the international agency's programs," said Joel. "Many times what we in the field believe is most essential—such as worldview training or strengthening marriages and families—is the hardest to fund because it doesn't fit exactly in the mandate of any of the international agencies."

So, how does the Nehemiah Center change this mindset? How can the Nehemiah Center convey to an organization's board—thousands of miles away—that its funding could be more effective if the organization was willing to collaboratively work with other organizations? It's a difficult path for Nehemiah Center staff members.

In the first chapter, Pastor Tomás Ruiz credited learning biblical worldview with the changes experienced by residents in Los Brasiles. In subsequent chapters, healthy marriage training helped

Lourdes Rivas and Alejandro Espinoza; an agricultural training and loan program helped Francisco Javier get his own farm; mission trips changed the life of Anna Van Rooselaar; Christian education gave Nery Martínez hope and a career; and support from a youth Bible study group got Nixon, a former gang member, off the streets. All stories of transformation.

These stories of transformation energize Nehemiah Center team members as they wrestle with the growing edges: funding, staffing, strategy, communication, and structure. As they wrestle, they also forge ahead confident that their focus on biblical worldview and collaboration is transforming the country around them.

For proof, they need only look at Pastor Diómedes Santeliz in Somotillo.

*The view from Diómedes Santeliz's Mountain of Prayer includes the border with Honduras.*

# 11

## Seeding Somotillo

*When I was introduced to biblical worldview, I understood that the church is the leader of the city, and should be involved in health, education, politics, in the most vulnerable parts of society.*

*-DIÓMEDES SANTELIZ*

Growing up in northern Nicaragua, Diómedes Santeliz had a poor but fairly typical home life. The fourth child in a Catholic family of twelve, Diómedes was raised in a rural village without electricity or any health facility. To get to school in Somotillo, he and three brothers walked five kilometers daily without shoes.

The story of his upbringing is not unlike that of many Nicaraguans.

Flash forward thirty years. See Diómedes' influence: Thirty-plus new churches, new preventative health programs, two new schools, a new agricultural training center, a new Christian radio station. Look at how area residents have transformed their marriages, their homes, and their churches. See how this agricultural area is learning irrigation techniques and watch residents experiment with new crops and new livestock.

What in the world happened here?

God in the world happened here.

"Diómedes is founding an NGO [non-governmental organization] to reach out to all denominations," said missionary Eric Loftsgard. "Essentially, he is creating a Nehemiah Center in his own zone."

## Time to Fish

As with most true transformations, the changes in Diómedes' life took place in tiny steps. The first step occurred after his older brother was killed in the political conflicts in the 1980s. A sympathetic teacher, who happened to be Baptist, helped the family, ultimately leading Diómedes to join the Baptist church and turn his life over to Christ. His own family, staunch Catholics, felt betrayed and kicked him out of the house.

Diómedes decided to stay in Somotillo, however, which at about 30,000 people, was the largest town in this area of northwest Nicaragua just a few miles from the Honduran border. He married and became a math teacher in the public school. In his free time, he helped out at his tiny Baptist church, sometimes preaching or playing the guitar for services.

When *Iglesia Bautista Príncipe de Paz* (Prince of Peace Baptist Church) asked him to be its full-time pastor, Diómedes agreed. At this point, his story again is similar to those we have heard before: he held services every night, but there was no growth. So, after two years, he resigned. A year later, the church had not found a new pastor, and Diómedes had not found a new job. When the congregation asked him to return, he consented, deciding that if nothing changed this time, he would leave both the pastorate and Somotillo.

At first, his frustration continued. He delegated responsibilities to church members, to no avail. He hosted prayer meetings; perhaps four members showed up. Before long, though, he began to sense an impending event, that God was telling him something was about to happen.

He did not anticipate that happening would be a hurricane.

When Hurricane Mitch hit, North American missionaries appeared with aid, modeling service in refugee camps. He and other church members joined them. They saw refugees accepting Christ, or, as Diómedes said, "at least praying a sinner's prayer of acceptance." The soil had been prepared for change.

In 1999, he received a flyer about an upcoming Managua biblical worldview conference, which included the words "seed projects." That caught his attention. "These are North Americans. Maybe they will give us seeds to plant," he thought. He prepared a list of needs, took baggage for transporting seeds, and headed for the conference.

And, paralleling the experience of countless others in previous chapters, learning about and really grasping the concepts of biblical worldview changed Diómedes' life.

"The conference was like God taking my brain and turning it around and putting it in the right position. It changed my life, my way of thinking. This was God's time for me."

Instead of receiving seed, Diómedes became one.

Hearing that Christians should work in the world was amazing, surprising, and inspiring.

"Now I could do something to help. [As a teacher,] I had taught, helped children, and had asked myself why the church is not invested with helping children. I had felt the church should be involved but wasn't convinced that was the right role for the church. So, this conference affirmed in my heart and put the fire in my heart to come back and preach what I had learned."

He returned to his church and gathered his members. Together, with help from what

Diómedes was learning from people associated with the Nehemiah Center, the church wrote its mission, vision, and values.

"And we prayed. Then I asked the church members to write on paper their ideas of what God was putting on their hearts, how we should be operating, supporting the community . . . We took all those ideas and put them together, and from there we talked and formed the vision."

This tiny church, which initially had only fifteen to twenty members, wrote an ambitious vision: Plant new churches in every community where there isn't one. Ensure that there is training within the new churches. Develop a Christian school that provides primary to university education. Build a medical clinic that can help with health issues in the community, not just curative but also preventative. Establish a health clinic to train health promoters for the community. The members even considered a radio station.

"And then we began to think, 'How do we get this new vision moving?' We wrote all that down."

They did more than write it down. By 2010, much of that vision had become reality. But getting from writing to reality required hard work. And, of course there were nay-sayers.

"In many other churches, pastors were preaching that the Trojan horse had arrived at the Baptist church," Diómedes remembered. One pastor took the initiative of opposing the new developments with public meetings, accusing the congregation and its pastor of heresy.

Within his own congregation, there were doubters. "I told the objectors, 'There are plenty of other churches who will receive you. Or, if you don't want that, start your own church, but what we want here is for the city to be for Christ and for the churches to preach to the community, not only to the congregation.'

"And then we took this purpose of the church and put it in one word: *Pescar*."

Pescar, which means "to fish" in Spanish became the acronym for the church's vision: Proclamation, Education, Service, Communion, Adoration, and Replication. Whatever the church members did, they kept in mind that they were fishing.

From the very beginning, the Nehemiah Center played a crucial part. "Any time a training was offered, I made sure to be involved," said Diómedes. "And so our vision, a lot of it came from inspiration of what was taught in the Nehemiah Center trainings. We are really a disciple of the Nehemiah Center.

"When we come up against difficulties, we have a good relationship with the Nehemiah Center so they can help with training in areas we are lacking. So, the trainings we then impart to staff and church members come with the transformational development."

*A Transformed Marriage*

Ablaze with a biblical worldview, one of those many training sessions Diómedes attended concerned healthy marriage. Diómedes and his wife, Claudia, have three children, ranging in age

FROM CAROL'S JOURNAL

## North American Miracle

Over dinner in a Somotillo restaurant, Pastor Diómedes Santeliz relaxes and tells us more about his life. He is a simple Nicaraguan, he says, used to a simple life. Once, though, he was selected to travel to North America for a pastoral conference.

With a little study, he had mastered the intricacies of the airplane lavatory. In the restroom adjacent the conference center of a five-star hotel, the learning curve steepened.

Ready to depart his cubicle, he looked for an appropriate flushing handle, but found none. He looked beside, behind, beneath. Still nothing.

He sat perplexed.

'I could not leave this stall as it was,' he says. 'People would think Nicaraguans were unsanitary idiots!'

So he raised his hands, looked heavenward, and prayed fervently, 'Lord, I don't know what to do. I have looked everywhere. I need a miracle. Please send a miracle.'

In faith, he stood up, and God sent a miracle. The toilet flushed!

He praised God profusely and returned to the meeting.

He tells us that only later did he learn that God performs this same miracle each time that stall is used.

from six to seventeen.

In time, Diómedes came to realize he had wasted the first five years of his marriage. "I missed the opportunity to enjoy that part of my life. I studied, taught, attended church, and held services every day. At night I made plans for classes—classes I was teaching and classes I was taking. I sometimes slept only from midnight to 1 a.m.

"I had no time for my wife. I had been taught pastors fasted, prayed, read the Bible. When you were fasting you couldn't be near your wife, not even touch her for the three days or week you were fasting. I did fasts of seven to twenty-one days, with only a dinner at night. And in this way, I lost the opportunity to be with my wife.

"I thank God my wife is a wonderful woman. She withstood much loneliness. It helped she was a daughter of the former pastor and knew the rigors of this life and didn't kick me out . . .

"I was stupid. I missed the best time and now I take advantage of every opportunity to be with her."

### A New School

In implementing its vision, the congregation began with a school, using the church building as a starting classroom. The first hurdle: no Christian teachers. They hired teachers, and within a year all three teachers had accepted Christ.

The only school in Somotillo at that point was the public school with multiple problems—teen pregnancy, drug use, HIV/AIDS. Parents concluded that a religious school would help their children learn values. Another thing that helped was that the church cleverly adopted its school name from that of a school in Managua considered to be one of the best: *Escuela Baptist Sea La Luz* (Be the Light Baptist School).

"The school gave us access to parents and youth with whom we could share the gospel," said Diómedes. "It was well received in the community."

The congregation persisted. North American missionaries who had come in the wake of Hurricane Mitch learned of the church's vision for a school and assisted with purchasing land. A Maryland Baptist congregation helped erect a building.

*Somotillo Christian secondary school*

In 2010, 430 students attended primary and secondary school in two different buildings. One hundred of these attended on scholarships sponsored by the organization, God of Second Chances Missions (a Tennessee-based, nonprofit Christian organization).

Touring the school grounds in 2010, Diómedes pointed to a piece of adjacent property where the congregation would like to build a vocational school. When he first inquired, the owner told him the price was $5,000, but later raised it to $15,000. "We are praying for a crisis in the owner's life so that he needs to sell the land," Diómedes said, smiling.

*New Churches*

Instead of having services every day, Diómedes closed his church three days a week and encouraged members to go into other communities. Those communities that were receptive essentially formed their own teams, who were discipled. After a while, those other communities chose the person with the greatest influence to be pastor, who was invited for additional training.

Ultimately, thirty-three communities created thirty-three new churches. "Now our church has a full-time missions person in charge of supervising the community pastors so everyone is working as a team," Diómedes said.

It is important to note that Diómedes' church saw its role not just in planting new churches but also encouraging those new churches to serve their communities, through programs such as Community Health Evangelism (CHE). Incidentally, Herberth Reyes and Elizabeth Rodríguez, who worked in El Ojoche to encourage its transformation (as discussed in Chapter 8), are members of the Somotillo church.

By January 2010, the church in Somotillo had grown to 250 regular members, and the church

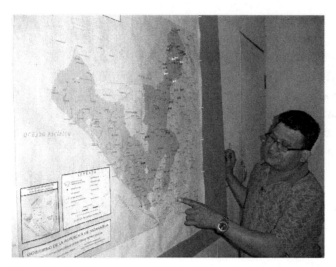

*Diómedes Santeliz uses a map to help plan his strategies for transformation.*

building could no longer accommodate the crowd. The church planned to move Sunday morning worship to the school auditorium and use the church space for smaller gatherings and midweek services.

### A New Agricultural Center

Looking at their surroundings, members of the church realized that agricultural training was also an urgent need. "We are a rural area," said Diómedes. "The communities outside of Somotillo live one hundred percent from agriculture. And they don't have any technical training how to improve their productivity."

With this vision and fervent prayer for partners, *Centro de Desarollo Integral Rural* (Center for Integrated Rural Transformation—CEDIR) was launched. Visiting North American teams, who learned about the vision for agricultural training on a piece of land adjacent to the current school, assisted with funding and building. A technical college in Managua agreed to provide agricultural teachers.

In 2009, the center had its first graduating class of forty-five students with a major in sustainable agricultural development. A second class of forty graduated in 2010. Graduates were from the northern six municipalities of the Chinandega province and one municipality in the León province.

In addition to formal schooling for youth, the center offers training for adult residents of area communities.

"God put it on our hearts that one way to reach farmers was to develop a technological demonstration farm to teach new technology and at same time share the gospel with them. If we were going to truly work in holistic development, we needed to work with all areas of life," said Diómedes. "If the pastors could produce agricultural products and provide for their families, it could be a good testimony for the families. That way a pastor has more influence in the community, connects with more people.

"That process is what I learned from the 'seed projects.' It was a different kind of seed. It is not about giving things to people. It is about training them to do things and be involved in their own lives."

When community representatives attend, they are trained in raising goats, sheep, chickens, or rabbits, and receive starter stock. They repay these loans with replacement animals when their stock give birth.

They also learn irrigation techniques and methods to raise new crops. There are strong local beliefs that certain plants, such as pineapple, will not grow in their climate. When students see it growing at the agricultural center, it is easier for them to be convinced. Following this vegetative training, students receive seeds and seedlings.

Submitted photo

*A group of pastors prays at the construction site of a new transmission tower for the Somotillo Christian radio station.*

### A Medical Clinic

Someday, church leaders hope to celebrate the opening of a medical clinic. It is part of the congregation's vision not yet fulfilled. In the meantime, Somotillo residents can take advantage of new preventative health programs. In addition to a medical clinic, Diómedes hopes to be able to provide technical training in nursing. He prays for a medical doctor, just into retirement, to work and help lead the medical center for a few years.

### A New Christian Radio Station

On the air from 5 a.m. to 10 p.m., the twenty-five-watt station had a sixty-kilometer broadcast radius in April 2011 and planned to triple that radius by July. Programming includes music, educational presentations, inspirational messages, and news—all compatible with the church's biblical worldview.

Its impact is far-reaching—even across the border into Honduras. One community there heard the broadcast, asked for discipleship training, received it, and has given birth to a daughter church.

FROM CAROL'S JOURNAL
*Mountains of Prayer*

FROM CAROL'S JOURNAL

*Mountains of Prayer*

As he talks of specific projects and dreams and goals, Diómedes often mentions praying about them. Intrigued, I ask about his personal prayer practices.

He spends an hour or more every morning in prayer, he tells me. He also sets aside one day each week for prayer and Bible study until four or five in the afternoon, when he turns to other activities. Diómedes not only owns Mountain of Prayer, he practices mountains of it: an hour per day and a day per week, while juggling a to-do list that astounds me.

I remember other Nicaraguans' stories: Daniel Aragón's daily 5 a.m. walk-and-pray time, Tomás Ruiz' all-night prayer sessions and days of fasting.

I think, even, of Martin Luther, "I have so much business I cannot get on without spending three hours daily in prayer."

I remember my tendency to skip right from rising to my to-do list when it gets long.

Why? I wonder. After all, I pay lip-service to the importance of prayer.

Is this commitment an advantage of the supernaturalist quality in Nicaraguan faith?

I wonder. I ponder these prayer practices in my heart.

And I wait for more data before I am willing to draw a conclusion.

I am, after all, still North American.

But then again . . .

## Dreams, Plans, and a Resignation

On the outskirts of Somotillo lies a small mountain—just five miles from the Honduran border. There is no real road to the top though it is passable by way of a four-wheel-drive vehicle. From its peak, one can see all of Somotillo. It was here, in the early 1980s, that the Sandinistas established a military outpost, watching their enemies and digging trenches for protection.

"This is our Mountain of Prayer," Diómedes said.

He has great dreams for this seven-acre parcel. He wants to convert the Sandinista trenches into houses for prayer—perhaps erecting small buildings atop those trenches where people can go for prayer and meditation. He wants to put a radio tower on top of the mountain and triple the reach of the radio station.

It is this mountain, too, that he dreams will be the future home for *Opportunidad Misionera Transformadora* (Opportunity for Transforming Mission), a nonprofit organization he is forming to continue the transformational work in his region.

Late in 2009, Diómedes resigned his position as a Baptist pastor because his vision now is broader than the Baptist denomination in which he has had impact throughout Nicaragua. He now sees he can have greater impact if he is not identified with one denomination. He hopes that ultimately, a Bible training center including a small seminary could also be part of his lofty mountaintop dream.

Through his experiences, he has come to realize that transformation means encouraging and empowering people to make their own interior transformations. He sees that reflected in his own vision.

"I'd like to tell you about something God has been putting on my heart from an interview of Billy Graham by Rick Warren. Rick Warren asked Billy Graham if he was reborn [that is, if he could start his life over again,] what he would do differently, and Billy Graham began to cry.

FROM CAROL'S JOURNAL

*Impossible Dream?*

For our last stop on our tour of Somotillo projects, our four-wheel-drive Mitsubishi Montero groans and spins its tires up a rocky slope as Diómedes talks of his vision for this mountain—houses of prayer, a radio tower, a seminary . . .

Earlier, I have listened as he talked of projects, rocking slightly in a wicker chair, shifting its angle from time to time in front of a pedestal fan. I have listened. I have believed.

But now, driving up this mountain as he shares more of his dreams, I think, but do not say, "This is a dream too big. Human dynamo that you are, this is too much even for you. Here your reach exceeds your grasp."

Then he tells me the details about the purchase of the mountain. When a Somotillo Christian—not a member of Diómedes' congregation—learned of the radio ministry, she offered to sell Diómedes this mountain for $16,000. She said she would donate a portion of what she received to her own church.

After she had made this offer to Diómedes, however, a government official offered her $60,000 for it, wanting to use its rock for building roads.

She asked Diómedes, "What should I do?" He suggested she honor her commitment to him. She said she would think it over.

She telephoned a week later. "I promised God to sell the land to you, so write the papers now, even if you can't pay right away. If I don't sign them now, I know I can't resist [the government offer]."

Diómedes tells me, "This assured me that this is a project of God."

Since that signing, the land has been paid for, electricity and water have been brought to the property, and the money has been secured to build the radio tower.

Hmmm.

Now, I remember Robert Browning's complete statement about reach and grasp: "Ah, but a man's reach should exceed his grasp,/ Or what's a heaven for?"

"Keep reaching, Diómedes," I think. "Keep reaching."

*Diómedes Santeliz kneels at old military marker where he is now planning a Mountain of Prayer.*

'After all I did in the crusades, I would have trained five other Billy Grahams. Now I am old. Who will follow with the same impact?' " Diómedes quoted Billy Graham as saying.

"That touched my heart. My focus is changing from the multitudes to training five, six, seven younger people to carry on with ministry. That is part of my decision to delegate the church pastoral role to someone else. If the Lord takes me home, there will be someone to carry on. That is love multiplication, and this is the time to do it. And that is where my greatest passion is now—to find these people and pour myself out for them."

Unlike the thick, black clay surrounding this area, the Somotillo people represent an organic soil, fertilized by training and collaboration, and watered by organizations in both Nicaragua and North America. The Somotillo people are doing much more than waiting for handouts. They are transformed and are agents of transformation—moving forward with vision and dreams and purpose, and collaborating with North American organizations to achieve those visions and dreams.

Twelve years ago, the seed that sprouted Somotillo's transformation was the transformation of Pastor Diómedes Santeliz. At that 1999 conference, he recognized for the first time what it meant to work for God in this world. He went back to his home and became like the seed planted in the good soil of Somotillo.

"Still other seeds fell on fertile soil, and they produced a crop that was thirty, sixty, and even a hundred times as much as had been planted!" (Matthew 13:8).

Where does Diómedes' dream end? Where does the Nehemiah Center's impact end? When does the transformation end?

In God's world: never.

# Postscript

It's August 2011, and I'm looking at my computer screen, ready to upload the book files to our printing company, click "submit," and generate the first copy of *On Mended Wings,* a tale born out of a search for a larger world that birthed in me a larger heart.

That sojourn lasted three years and filled my office and Donna's with fifteen books and two feet of paper files. Together, we also have 373 electronic folders, which contain 6,203 files, 2,271 of them photos. Undeleted emails total 1,395. We haven't counted hours; we didn't want to. This has been, after all, a journey of love.

When I click "submit," the journey ends. Or does it?

Under its 2011-2015 plan, the Nehemiah Center continues collaborating and transforming brokenness in new locations in Nicaragua.

Joel Huyser, one of its cofounders, is applying his passion for networking to other countries and continents. Earlier this year, Joel traveled to three countries in Asia to learn more about what God has been doing in that part of the world. Joel says, "Everywhere in the world there is a great need for grassroots Christians to join hands to bring Gospel-sized transformation to their neighborhoods, cities, and nations." He continues to assist churches with ending the false division between sacred and secular and with working together as a body across the differences of denomination, culture, race, and vocation.

North American teams continue to visit the Nehemiah Center and return home, challenged to be the change they hope to see in their own hometowns. Three North American congregations—including my home congregation—take faltering first steps in their commitments to walk alongside companion churches in Nicaragua.

As for me, recently retired from active work at the business I founded, I'm an adolescent again—wondering what I will be in this new phase of life. I'm energized by the possibility of helping my congregation flesh out its new relationship with Chinandega churches. I'd like to return to Nicaragua a month each year, to serve and to learn. Who knows? Perhaps I'll find another pocket of God-at-work somewhere on the globe to explore and then share with others.

Released to soar, *On Mended Wings* begins life on its own, accompanied by our hopes and prayers that its stories of transforming grace will challenge readers toward their own searching and journeying, to whatever square inch of the earth Jesus calls them.

After all, a journey may end, but the growing of a heart goes on forever.

*Carol Van Klompenburg*

PS: Readers who would like to share their own stories of searching, journeying, and growing hearts may email the authors at: onmendedwings.2@gmail.com. Readers wanting to explore options for service and learning at the Nehemiah Center may email: info@nehemiahcenter.net.

# Appendix A
## International Agencies Working with the Nehemiah Center

There are eight international agencies that regularly collaborate with the Nehemiah Center. These agencies are essential to the work. Not only do these organizations provide crucial funding support, but they also often provide missionaries, volunteers, and other support in a multitude of ways.

**Collaborating agencies include:**
- Caribbean Ministries Association
- Christian Reformed World Missions
- Christian Reformed World Relief Committee
- EduDeo
- Food for the Hungry
- Global CHE Enterprises
- Missionary Ventures International
- Partners Worldwide
- Worldwide Christian Schools

Agency descriptions on the pages that follow are taken from each agency's Web site.

The Nehemiah Center is always seeking new international partners. For more information on how you can participate in the collaborative work of this community, send an email to info@nehemiahcenter.net. More information is also available at the Nehemiah Center Web site: www.nehemiahcenter.net.

# Caribbean Ministries Association
### *(www.missioncma.com)*

We exist to provide Biblical training to serve the churches and ministries in and around the Caribbean. We are committed to teaching Scripture's foundational doctrines; that the people of God may be fully equipped to rightly divide the Word of Truth.

The vision of Caribbean Ministries Association is to empower the churches of the Caribbean by providing an interdenominational Bible training ministry, establishing and equipping God's people in God's Word.

The Caribbean is home to over 40 million people, many of whom have heard the Gospel but have only nominal spiritual growth. Churches are numerous, yet skilled teaching and training for the people is limited. Most churches are pastored by lay ministers who have had little opportunity to receive formal Bible training. Equipping these leaders will impact their congregations and generations to come through the Word of God.

For most of these lay pastors and church leaders to leave their homes and churches to attend seminary abroad is not only cost prohibitive, but would leave their churches without a pastor for an extended period of time. These leaders need equipping opportunities in the Caribbean that will allow them to continue their ministry while receiving the training that they need.

# Christian Reformed World Missions

*(www.crcna.org/pages/crwm.cfm)*

Established on June 18, 1888, by the Christian Reformed Church (CRC), Christian Reformed World Missions (CRWM) is a missions agency that helps CRC congregations to fulfill the Great Commission. CRWM partners with nearly 1,100 CRC congregations in Canada and the United States as well as with organizations and individuals around the world to proclaim the Gospel, promote healthy churches, and to do our part in extending the reign of Christ.

CRWM has missionaries serving in more than 20 countries and, through partnerships, our work extends to more than 40 countries.

**Key strategies include:**
- Working with global networks and movements to advance the reign of Christ
- Mobilizing CRC congregations for greater missions involvement
- Strengthening Christians in the CRC of North America and its international partners

**Mission:**
CRWM exists to glorify God by helping the CRC to respond obediently to our Lord's commission to witness to the good news of God's Kingdom and make disciples of all nations.

**Vision**:
We see the CRCNA vigorously participating in Spirit-led mission with churches and other Christian organizations throughout the world so that together we are proclaiming the gospel to more and more people who have not heard it, healthy churches are emerging and the Kingdom of God is advancing.

# Christian Reformed World Relief Committee

*(www.crwrc.org)*

The Christian Reformed World Relief Committee (CRWRC) is the relief and development arm of the Christian Reformed Church. CRWRC reaches out in God's name to people, both in North America and around the world, who are struggling with poverty, hunger, disaster, and injustice to help them find lasting ways to improve their lives.

One aspect of this ministry is community development. In this ministry CRWRC's staff members engage in community transformation in 30 countries around the world. They partner with more than 130 churches and community organizations to train local people to be leaders in their own communities. Together, CRWRC and these partners help people work together to overcome illiteracy, hunger, malnutrition, unemployment, HIV/AIDS, child mortality, injustice, and other issues affecting them.

Another aspect of CRWRC's ministry is disaster response and relief. When disasters strike, CRWRC responds to the urgent needs that arise. In North America, this often includes clearing debris, assessing needs, training local leaders, and repairing and rebuilding damaged homes. Internationally, it includes providing and distributing emergency food, water, shelter, and other supplies. It also often involves reconstruction of homes and livelihoods.

The third aspect of CRWRC's ministry involves working with people in North America and around the world to connect them to ministry, deepen their understanding of global issues, and encourage them to act and advocate on behalf of those in need.

**Mission Statement**

CRWRC's mission is to engage God's people in redeeming resources and developing gifts in collaborative acts of love, mercy, justice, and compassion.

# EduDeo Ministries
*www.edudeo.com*

**Vision:** Every community transformed by the Gospel

**Mission:** To advance Christ-centred education for children worldwide.

EduDeo Ministries (formally Worldwide Christian Schools-Canada) is a Canadian, Christian, mission organization serving children in developing countries with quality education rooted in a Biblical worldview. Their strategic approach includes accessibility for all children, teacher training, curriculum development, and school construction. They promote sustainable schools by partnering long-term with school associations and mission organizations that share their vision.

EduDeo partners with the Nehemiah Center in the area of Christian education, working with ACECEN (the association of Christian schools in Nicaragua) to train teachers and administrators in how to develop an integral, Biblical perspective in their schools. It has become quickly apparent that one of the most effective ways to bring about lasting change is through quality education with a distinctly Christian worldview. EduDeo also assists schools involved with ACECEN in building and improving their facilities through financial resources and volunteers.

# Food for the Hungry

*(www.fh.org)*

Food for the Hungry was founded in 1971 and gave birth to the ministry now at work in more than 26 countries worldwide. Since then, Food for the Hungry has boldly spoken out for and served the poor, sending courageous heroes to help communities transform themselves. Founder Dr. Larry Ward held to the simple premise that "they die one at a time, and so we can help them one at a time."

**Mission:**

> To walk
> with churches, leaders and families
> in overcoming all forms of human poverty
> by living in healthy relationship with God and His creation.

Food for the Hungry embraces an intensely personal and biblical response to God's call to end physical and spiritual hungers worldwide. This intentional walk with the poor mirrors God's walk with each of us, recognizing our own brokenness and His transforming grace that brings out our God-given potential.

**Vision:**

> God called
> and we responded
> until physical and spiritual hungers ended worldwide.

In response to His call, and compelled by the love of Christ, Food for the Hungry goes to the hard places – places darkened by poverty, war and injustice – to bring hope and help to children, families and communities in the most impoverished countries around the world.

# Global CHE Enterprises
## *(www.globalche.org)*

Community Health Evangelism (CHE) is a best practices model for integrating evangelism and discipleship with community-based development. CHE originated in Africa in the 1980s. As CHE developed as a ministry strategy and its ability to transform communities become apparent, it spread around the world. Today CHE is being used by churches, denominations, mission agencies, non-government organizations, and national and local governments in more than 75 nations to lift whole communities out of cycles of poverty and disease.

The purpose of Community Health Evangelism is not just breaking poverty or planting churches, though both of those things are accomplished through CHE. The real goal of our work is a transformation in lives and communities that is as deep as the human heart, and as broad as the whole range of the human experience in the world God made. We want Jesus to be recognized as Lord over all creation, and our development activities reflect the depth and breadth of the kingdom of God. We are asking God to work in us and through us to transform beliefs and change behavior so that His peace, justice, compassion, and righteousness are reflected in the life of the communities we serve.

CHE seamlessly integrates evangelism, discipleship, and church planting with community health and development. The ministry is holistic, seeking to obey everything that Jesus commanded and addressing the whole need of individuals and communities.

**The vision of Global CHE Enterprises is two-fold:**
- To see individuals encounter the living God through the actions of the body of Christ so that they are changed from the inside out and in turn enable God to work through them so that their communities are transformed.
- To lead individuals and Christian organizations worldwide to initiate and strengthen ministries that lead people to become followers of Jesus and lift whole communities out of cycles of poverty and disease.

**The mission:**
Global CHE Enterprises brings hope to impoverished rural and urban communities through sharing the Good News of the Gospel, preventing disease, and engaging in wholistic community-based development.

# Missionary Ventures International
## *(www.mvi.org)*

Our Vision: Involving People to Impact Nations for Christ

Our Mission: MVI seeks to empower, equip, and encourage indigenous churches and leaders to reach their own people with the love and message of Jesus.

Our Strategy: MVI exists to serve and support the indigenous church. Our aim is to have key strategic partnerships to see their God-given visions fulfilled.

Our Workers: MVI facilitates personal involvement in missions by partnering with churches, groups and individuals to encourage and enable their missionary involvement.

Our Goal: MVI desires to see healthy indigenous churches and programs which are self-governing. Through a balance of limited support, investment and mentoring, over time the churches and projects become strong and self-sustaining. Finally, we encourage churches to look beyond their own situations and reach out to other parts of the world with the Great Commission and the Great Commandment.

**How do we work?**

In most countries the work is pioneered by our long-term missionaries who we call Field Coordinators. They form key relationships, develop outreach plans, host short-term teams, oversee new projects and ensure that donated funds are used effectively and with integrity.

**Core values:**
- The Great Commandment and the Great Commission
- Facilitating Indigenous Missions
- Personal Involvement
- Interdenominational Ministry
- Spirit-Led Ministry
- Mutual Cooperation and Unity Through Relationships
- Uncompromising Biblical Culture

# Partners Worldwide
## *(www.partnersworldwide.org)*

**Who We Are**

A Movement: Partners Worldwide is a dynamic global network of business and professional people who bear witness to their faith and love in Jesus Christ so that rich and poor, individuals and groups, communities and nations are transformed to more completely reflect the kingdom of God.

Business as Mission: We believe that God has uniquely equipped and placed businesspeople to use their skills and experience to be agents of transformation within their own businesses, in their communities, and around the world.

Part of the Solution: We recognize that businesspeople are gifted and positioned to respond to the challenges of global poverty with enterprising, empowering solutions.

**Our Focus**

Partners Worldwide walks alongside business leaders who have servant hearts, a kingdom focus, and a passion for a world without poverty.

In the countries where we work we partner with local business champions and networks that care about their communities, know the business environment, and can build on the local resources.

We engage and support our network of businesspeople through global partnerships and personal relationships that transform the lives of all involved. We provide a framework for healthy cross-cultural partnerships, vibrant networking, and shared learning opportunities. We promote models and tools for success and sustainability—including training, mentoring, access to capital, and advocacy tools.

We encourage our partnerships to focus on the small and medium business sector—the "missing middle" in the developing world. These are businesses that have made, or have the potential to make, the jump from an informal micro enterprise to a formal small to medium enterprise (SME).This sector, which faces some of the greatest challenges in the developing world, is underserved yet has amazing potential for impacting poverty through job creation and leadership.

**Mission**

Encourage, equip and connect business and professional people in global partnerships that grow enterprises and create sustainable jobs, transforming the lives of all involved.

# Worldwide Christian Schools

*(www.wwcs.org)*

Worldwide Christian Schools (WWCS) is a non-denominational, evangelical ministry whose mission is to assist other responsible Christian organizations in developing Christ-centered schools throughout the world. Our vision is to ensure that all children have access to Christ-centered education.

WWCS does not own or operate schools. Instead, we work through nationally-led partners to establish, maintain and expand Christ-centered schools wherever they are needed most, primarily in the developing world. WWCS promotes schools that have ACCESS:

- Accountability
- Christ-centered worldview
- Community leadership
- Education for teachers
- Sustainability
- Steady Improvement

Worldwide Christian Schools Canada changed its name to EduDeo Ministries in June 2011. Both Worldwide Christian Schools and EduDeo Ministries remain close and continue to collaborate where it makes sense.

# Appendix B
## Nehemiah Center Vision, Mission, and Core Values

**Identity**

The Nehemiah Center is a multicultural community of learning, service, and collaboration, comprised of three teams: an international team, an administrative support team, and a training and consulting team composed of Nicaraguan leaders (the Ezra team).

**Vision**

We see individuals, churches, organizations, and local communities who are putting into practice the values of a biblical worldview and who are learning, serving, and collaborating together for the transformation of both their own lives and the broader society.

**Mission**

To develop integral agents of transformation who are grounded in a Christ-centered, biblical worldview and woven into local, vocational, and global networks of learning, service, and collaboration for the transformational development of communities and nations.

**Core Values**

- *Biblical worldview*: an orientation to life that views the world from the holistic perspective of God's good creation, which although contaminated by human sin, is being reconciled to God through Jesus Christ. The role of the church is to be a sign and ambassador of this reconciliation by seeking Christ's Lordship in all aspects of life. We desire the renewal of all areas of society both in Nicaragua and in other countries based on a biblical worldview. We believe that a biblical worldview transforms individuals, families, churches, and neighborhoods as well as business, education, and professional life.

- *Holistic transformational development:* a process through which communities learn to take responsibility for their own lives and resolve their own problems based on a biblical worldview and grounded in God's purposes for their lives. Holistic transformational development results in fresh knowledge and ideas, justice and peace in social relationships, the development of new resources and adequate material well-being, as well as spiritual growth and leadership development in local churches.

- *Equipping agents of transformation*: the identification of people who are trustworthy, available, and teachable and who, as a result of intensive training along with long-term mentoring and discipling, commit themselves to actively participate as partners in the realization of the Kingdom of God on earth as well as in heaven. We follow the example of Jesus who invested three years in twelve disciples who in turn changed the world. We practice and promote primarily the methodologies of adult education in all our training.

- *Collaboration:* among Christians from different denominations, organizations, and nationalities who share the core values of the Nehemiah Center. Our mission is to serve other leaders and organizations with the purpose of broadening their vision and encouraging their collaboration in achieving the goal of transformational development. We promote a collaboration based on a biblical worldview between churches of different denominations, different organizations, between and among the different areas of society, and between people and organizations from different countries.

- *Team work*: the interchange between people with different gifts and abilities leads to the synergy that is necessary for development. Development requires new ways of doing things that are motivated by a diversity of ideas and actions at various levels.

- *Servant leadership:* Jesus is our model of service and shows us how to be of influence in the lives of people and communities. We begin by humbly recognizing the gifts and skills that we and others have, as well as acknowledging our own weaknesses. We aspire to grow towards the fullness of Christ.

- *Persistent prayers of confession, repentance, and intercession for our communities and nation:* The restoration of a community or nation is always accompanied by confession, repentance, and intercession. This was also the example of Nehemiah in Nehemiah 1:5-11.

- *Training and development of local leaders*: holistic transformational development must be owned by the community itself. We seek to equip and empower leaders in local communities, modeling servant leadership.

- *Transparency and stewardship in the use and management of finances:* We begin with the truth that all money belongs to God and that we should administer our resources in a just and prudent manner. We will implement financial policies that require transparency, including an annual independent audit.

- *Renewal of the family, school, business, government, and local church:* The sustainable development of the community requires the renewal and strengthening of each of these basic sectors of the society and their restoration to the original purposes of God.

# Appendix C
## Additional Resources

For more information about Nicaragua or about transformational changes, here are some additional resources you may wish to consult:

**Books**

Berman, Joshua and Wood, Randall. *Moon Living Abroad in Nicaragua*. Avalon Travel. Berkeley, California. 2010.

Berman, Joshua and Wood, Randall. *Moon Nicaragua*. Avalon Travel. Berkeley, California. 2010.

Corbett, Steve and Fikkert, Brian. *When Helping Hurts: How to Alleviate Poverty without Hurting the Poor . . . and Yourself.* Moody Publishers. Chicago, Illinois. 2009.

Corbitt, J. Nathan and Nix-Early, Vivian. *Taking It to the Streets: Using the Arts to Transform Your Community.* Baker Books. Grand Rapids, Michigan. 2003.

Kinzer, Stephen. *Blood of Brothers: Life and War in Nicaragua.* Putnam Publishing Group. New York, New York. 1991.

Livermore, David A. *Serving with Eyes Wide Open: Doing Short-Term Missions with Cultural Intelligence.* Baker Books. Grand Rapids, Michigan. 2006.

Miller, Darrow L. with Guthrie, Stan. *Discipling Nations: The Power of Truth to Transform Cultures.* YWAM Publishing. Seattle, Washington. 2001.

Moffitt, Bob. *If Jesus Were Mayor: How Your Local Church Can Transform Your Community.* Monarch Books. 2007.

Myers, Bryant. *Walking with the Poor: Principles and Practices of Transformational Development.* Orbis Books. Maryknoll, New York. 1999.

Seebeck, Doug and Stoner, Timothy. *My Business, My Mission: Fighting Poverty Through Partnerships.* Partners Worldwide. Grand Rapids, Michigan. 2009.

Senge, Peter M. *The Fifth Discipline: The Art and Practice of the Learning Organization.* Doubleday. New York, New York. 1990.

Smith, James K.A. *Desiring the Kingdom: Worship, Worldview, and Cultural Formation.* Baker Academic. Grand Rapids, Michigan. 2009.

Van Dyke, John. *The Craft of Christian Teaching: A Classroom Journey.* Dordt Press. Sioux Center, Iowa. 2005.

Walker, Thomas W. *Nicaragua: Living in the Shadow of the Eagle.* Westview Press. Boulder, Colorado. 2003.

Wright, Christopher J.H. *The Mission of God's People; A Biblical Theology of the Church's Mission.* Zondervan. Grand Rapids, Michigan. 2010.


**Web Sites**

Center for Transforming Mission (www.ctmnet.org)

Disciple Nations Alliance (www.disciplenations.org)

Harvest Foundation (www.harvestfoundation.org)

# About the Authors

*Carol Van
Klompenburg*

*Donna Biddle*

Carol Van Klompenburg is founder and owner of The Write Place (www.thewriteplace.biz). She has written articles, plays, and books, and has taught nonfiction writing at two Iowa colleges. She has an MA in Theatre Arts from the University of Minnesota and a BA in English from Dordt College.

From 2008 to 2011, while she did research for *On Mended Wings,* she and her husband, Marlo, made four trips from their home in Pella, Iowa, to Nicaragua. In 2008, after committing to regular volunteer work in Nicaragua, they also became struggling students of Spanish.

*On Mended Wings* is Carol's seventh book and the second one she has co-authored with Donna Biddle, of Kearney, Nebraska. A graduate of the University of Missouri School of Journalism, Donna covered politics for more than ten years as a newspaper reporter, then worked in corporate communications, before joining The Write Place in 1999. In 2008, the authors published *In Search of a Better Way: The Lives and Legacies of Gary and Matilda Vermeer.*

CPSIA information can be obtained at www.ICGtesting.com
Printed in the USA
LVOW051308021111

253185LV00003B/1/P